A Dangerous Book for Dogs

Train Your Humans -- The Bandit Method

OTHER TITLES
From Cathy Burnham Martin

Dog Days in the Life of the Miles-Mannered Man

Healthy Thinking Habits: Seven Attitude Skills Simplified

Of the Same Blood: Your Eurasian Heritage

Sage, Thyme & Other Life Seasonings: Perspectives

Fifty Years of Fabulous Family Favorites, Volumes 1-3

Champagne! Facts, Fizz, Food & Fun

Boat Drinks

Dockside Dining: Round One

Dockside Dining: A Second Helping

Dockside Dining: Back for Thirds

Cranberry Cooking

Lobacious Lobster

The Communication Coach:
Business Communication Tips from the Pros

A Dangerous Book for Dogs
Train Your Humans – The Bandit Method

Per the paws of
Bandit

Assisted by his human,
Cathy Burnham Martin

Quiet Thunder Publishing
Manchester, NH

QUIET THUNDER PUBLISHING

www.QTPublishing.com

This title and more are featured at
www.GoodLiving123.com

A Dangerous Book for Dogs

Train Your Humans – The Bandit Method

Full color edition: ISBN 978-1-939220-13-4
Black & white paperback edition: ISBN 978-1-939220-32-5
eBook edition: ISBN 978-1-939220-33-2
Audiobook edition: ISBN 978-1-939220-14-1

Published and printed in the United States of America.

Library of Congress Control Number: 2016930518

TABLE OF CONTENTS

FREE EXTRA TREATS:
(Because you've been good!)
#1 Food & Treat Safety
#2 More Secrets to Happiness
#3 Great Resources
#4 Careers for Dog Lovers

Acknowledgements

More Photos for My Fans

WARNING

It is of vital importance that this book does NOT land in human paws! You may share it with all your canine pals, of course. (Your feline friends may also enjoy gleaning a few tips.) However, when you have completed your program, we strongly suggest eating or destroying this book. Chomp it down, hide it under a large piece of furniture, bury it in the back yard, shred it into tiny bits and scatter them all over the house, or take any other steps necessary to prevent your humans from catching onto your secrets! (My buddy, Allen, asked if the pages of my book were dog-eared. Ha ha. The answer is, "No." But I will slurp them down rather than let a human get a taste of this Top Secret Info.)

ABOUT THE AUTHOR

Bandit Burnham Martin is a Thanksgiving pup. A Maltipoo from the Best of Breed Puppy Farm in Zephyrhills, Florida, he started life as the runt of his litter. While the Maltipoo standard is white or champagne, he sported black hair with a strong cinnamon undercoat. A pure cinnamon band crossed his eyes forming a mask of sorts, inspiring the name Bandit. His dark hair grew out pure white, but it later began changing, revealing a snazzy tri-color coat.

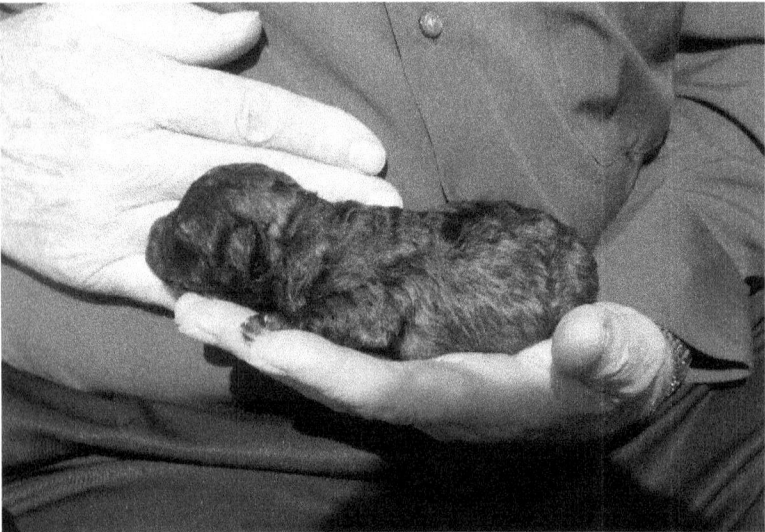

His Bandit name gained more significance as he quickly grew into a notorious thief. He continues to steal hearts and kisses as often as possible.

Though he'd never be the standard 10-to-12-pound Maltipoo, his enormous spirit and effervescent personality boosted his stature to Super Dog. Further supporting this image shines his early friendship with Miles, a Newfoundland. While Bandit is physically the size of his best buddy's head, these two bonded quickly. Thanks to Miles' influence, Bandit has never considered himself a small dog in any way.

In fact, there have been whispers that Bandit is also actually a Newfie himself. As part of the Canine Witness Protection Program, his Maltipoo appearance provides a pawsitively perfect disguise for this very special Furrever Dog.

DEDICATION

I dedicate this book to my Poppy and Mom Burnham, my very first humans, who were always so very gentle, patient and loving... plus to all the many friends who have meandered in and out of my life. I have been so blessed to know many wonderful people... and pups, too! Okay, and my very own kitty, Jeeter.

INTRODUCTION 🐾

Humans are really great people, but they can be a little slow. I mean, it can take a lifetime to train them. Regardless, I decided as a mere pup to make training my humans my life's work.

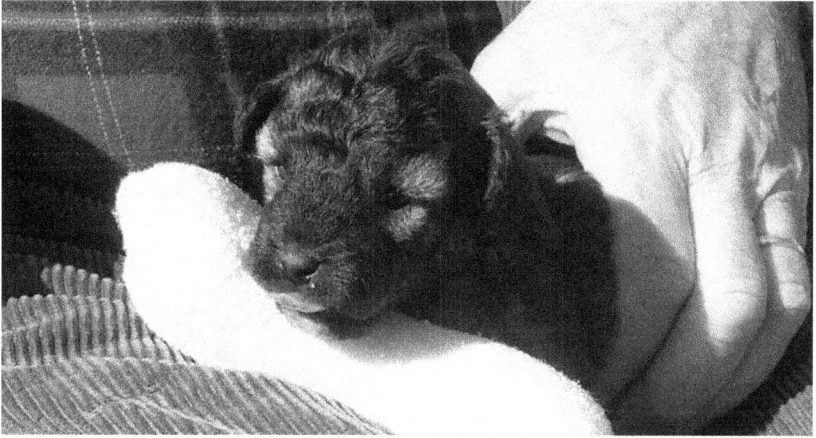

As a tiny, wee lad

I guess that's how I became a doggone expert, because I've got my humans superbly trained, if I do say so myself. And I do say so! Even other humans are impressed with how well I have them trained.

It was a natural progression for me to branch out officially, with The Bandit Method, and just keep on keeping on. Years ago I lost count of how many humans I've trained. The number includes virtually every human I've ever met.

I worked with my first humans, Bob and Glenna Burnham, on several important skills. Big yard, little yard, down, bring it, paws up, no speak, night-night, dog, and cookie to name just a few.

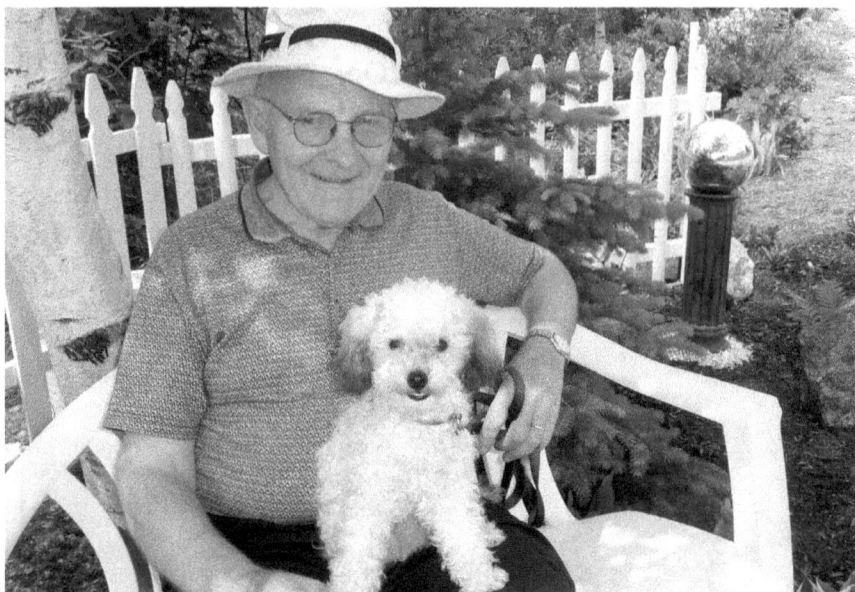

Hanging out with my first Poppy

Later, when they moved into an apartment that wouldn't allow dogs, I moved in with their daughter, Cathy, and her husband, The Ronald Martin. Oh, yeah, I had to start retraining my humans all over again. I've learned a lot about doing this. No problem.

With pleasure, I now share my experiences, human training exercises, best kept secrets, and tales of silly human misadventures... all chronicled for you here in these pages. Simply apply these tips on your own humans and make all of us dog-gone proud!

It's not as difficult as we canines sometimes think. The Bandit Method shows you exactly how to do this, without medication, expensive training DVDs, weeks of lessons, creepy training collars, electronic fences, baby gates, or even a leash for your humans. Trust me! I'm a dog!

Oh, and though we do indeed think, don't worry about confusing your humans with your deepest thoughts. Just tilt your head in standard listening fashion, and let them keep thinking that we don't think.

So, come on! Give me a high paw. Devour this information like your favorite cookie or your human's favorite shoe. You can do it!

1

UNDERSTANDING HUMANS

Before you can truly train your humans, you need to understand them. This is no small task. Throughout the book, I will try to provide helpful insights.

For example, we see things sooooo differently. Ours is a flavorful, scent-filled, excitement-packed, zig-zag world. Theirs is more controlled. Straight lines are important, and they miss way too much of the fun, way too often. One of our major responsibilities is helping our humans to live more fully and enjoyably. Thankfully, for canines this comes naturally.

To add insight, consider this description of one of my recent simple, daily adventures.

I head out the back door into the wilds of the deep, dark forest that lies beyond the lawn. At the far edge of the grass, I pause for a moment to look back at my house…my last vestige of security. Sigh. My human is standing in the open doorway watching me. I quietly hope this will not be the last time I see her face. But Life is uncertain, at best. Who knows what lies just ahead of me?

Undaunted, I head out on the dangerous trek through the landscaping rocks and plants. I pause briefly to sniff each one, making certain that my territory has not been compromised. Then my wilderness adventure truly begins. (Uh, cue the dramatic music, please.)

I enter the deep, dark woods and listen to the mournful whine of the many salivating predators watching me. I am big. I am bold. I am invincible! (Okay, okay… I am seven pounds of fun, fur and fury, but I'm in the middle of a story here.)

Suddenly, a giant, cranky serpent leaps up in my path. Woah! I instinctively dart to one side, averting sure destruction. That was close, but I'm not out of danger yet. The trees tower over me, looming, leering, and laughing, stretching their "craggly" arms and fingers in all directions, trying to snag me. Some crazy, prehistoric bird swoops over me, and I deftly duck out of the way, cleverly eluding capture yet again. Crazy!

I stealthily press onward. (Okay, okay… I scamper.) I stoop to slip under a massive fallen tree trunk and then curve cautiously around a giant stump, pausing to admire a delirious butterfly, obviously sent to distract me from my vital mission of exploration. I zig. I zag. I cavort. I am big. I am HUGE! I am brave. I… am… invincible!!

Boom – boom - boom – boom. (Uh, I've added a little timpani to the orchestration here... just to muffle the pounding of my heart.)

Half a dozen leaf-like monsters simultaneously leap and swirl about me. They are trying to bewilder and confuse me. I will not have my mission thwarted by these beasts. I am focused on finding the lions and tigers and bears, after all.

First, I must cross this mighty ocean that looms now before me. It stretches further than the eye can see in all directions. This could be my greatest challenge.

In the far distance behind me, I hear the human calling to me. Oh, no. Not now. I am so close to the center of adventure, I must not be distracted or diverted from my task. I remain on point. I pretend I hear nothing. I sniff. I mark. I move on.

I must conquer these uncharted territories for all canines and creatures large and small. I am big. I am brave. I am INVINCIBLE!

"Cookie!"

Oops! I heard the magic word from my human. Conquering the world will have to wait. As a dog I must miss no opportunity to score a treat. I zoom in as straight a line as canine-ly possible. A cookie awaits me!!

Now... what I have just told you is what really happened. Yet, I heard my human telling the tale, and I could hardly believe my ears. Let me share with you how little she remembered of my great adventure. And she is my best eye witness? Good grief.

"Bandit went out the back door, as usual. He crossed the lawn and did his business in the border garden. Then, he turned back to see if I was really watching. I told him to come, but he ignored me and headed into the trees. I watched him step on a little twig on the ground, and he got totally startled as it flipped up toward him. A tiny chickadee almost landed right beside him, but his jumping scared it. Then Bandit batted at a couple of leaves that a breeze picked up and swirled around his head. I gave up calling his name. As he approached the big puddle of collected rainwater, I simply called out the word "cookie." Bandit did an immediate about face and raced straight up the 20 feet to the lawn. He leapt up onto the deck, skipping the steps completely. Anything for a cookie."

Well, she got the "anything for a cookie" part right.

We all must teach our humans that simple commands like "Come" are way less effective than "Cookie." With training, your human can learn to kick it up to that most wonderful of 2-syllable words, too.

Anyway, here's the point. Humans just don't see the world the way we do, so we must be persistent and patient while training them. Don't miss any opportunities for reinforcement either.

For instance, even when I'm just a tiny distance apart from her on the lawn, and she calls to me, I immediately recognize a training or reinforcement opportunity. She says, "Bandit. Come." I dutifully stop, turn around, and look at her. She repeats, "Bandit. Come."

If you are doing this, pay attention: Your next action is verrrry important. Do NOT move. Again, this is the most vital step. Do not move even one muscle.

Look at your human with love and encouragement. No matter how many times they command, clap their hands or even whistle, simply sit and look at them. You can tilt your head to the side, of course. This lets them know that you are paying close attention and trying to understand their feeble attempt at communication.

The moment they offer the treat by calling out, "Cookie," run as fast as possible to them. Wear your most gleeful face. Then sit dutifully by their feet or by your food dish and grin until they deliver the hard-earned treat. You are teaching them. And they did well.

See, it's all about attitude. And patience. Your human can do this... and more! Give them a big kiss when they do it right!

Okay, let's move on... we have so many lessons and so little time. Zoom zoom!

2

CH-CH-CH-CHANGES

Part of transitioning from understanding to training our humans is to recognize that they are all different, and yet very much the same. We need to start by helping them learn some resilience.

We tend to go with the flow… It's canine nature. Humans tend to resist change… It's human nature. We need to help them see the good in change and to embrace it. It wastes so much energy to fight things that are inevitable. That just stresses us out and drains us, not to mention causing us to miss out on some things that could be good. While it's not always easy, we need to help our humans see change as the next wonderful adventure.

For example, we all can have a bad day from time to time. I am no different, and I'll never forget my toughest day. Woof! It turned into my toughest year. But I set the example of resilience for my humans.

They were moving into a senior citizen independent living facility in Florida. At the time, the management just didn't know how much love and enthusiasm I inspire in humans. Their policy prohibited me from sleeping there! (Bad humans! They needed more training and encouragement.)

Anyway, my human Mom and Dad, who have loved me one thousand percent since I was born, had to give me to their daughter. My Cathy human and her husband, The Ronald, would adopt me.

After so many trips to and from airports, one more was no big deal. However, *this* time was very different.

Mom and Dad were standing on the sidewalk crying their eyes out with my Cathy human. Wow! Something really bad was happening. I had never seen this before. They all just kept crying and hugging each other. Turns out that my folks were just soooo sad to have to give me up. They were also very glad that I could stay with family. Mixed feelings are so confusing for our humans.

You see, my crazy Cathy human is the one who had found me for my folks in the first place. Well now, here we were again. It was April first, but this was no April Fool's Day joke. This was moving on time for my folks and me!

I'm a great frequent flyer, so the trip to my new home was a piece of cake. My Cathy human and her husband, The Ronald, were already great buddies of mine. I always loved visiting their house, especially to see my very first best-buddy dog, who lived there, too.

I guess my Mom had tried to tell me when "it" had happened, but I just didn't understand. My pal was old and hadn't made it past New Year's. Sigh. I couldn't believe it.

I had to see for myself. We come zooming up the road from the airport. I recognized every tree! Yippee! When I went tearing into the house, I zipped straight into the kitchen where I knew he'd be sleeping on his bed. Nope, not there.

I snooped about a bit, but he wasn't inside. When they let me out the back door, I made a beeline for his apartments… those snazzy holes he'd dug under the sun porch. No way!

He wasn't hiding on me either. This was no game. It was very sad. He was such a big-hearted ol' lug. I'm gonna miss the guy something fierce.

There's nothing quite like a 7-pound Maltipoo hanging out with his 100-plus-pound Newfoundland buddy. (Yeah, he used to joke with me that his head weighed more than my entire body. He was always a real wise guy.) I'll see him again someday. I just have to be very patient.

So, I lost my parents, my home, and my best buddy all on the same day. On the other hand, I will see my parents when they visit and when I travel.

I now live in a new home that I already know very well, I've got great step-humans, and I'm meeting some wonderful new buddies. See, we pooches know how to bounce back. We must always set a great example for our humans, because they tend to adapt more slowly.

Jeeter, my kitty

Living in my new home is a cat named Jeeter. He is twice as big as I am! No joke! Jeeter purrs reeeeeally loudly. It's rather comforting.

He may take a while to get used to me. I think I just have a little too much energy for him. So, right this minute, he's a little scared of me, but I'll get him over that in a blink!

Jeeter and Daisy

My Grandma Martin, who was living with us when I moved in, has a Black Labrador dog she rescued as a pup. Her name is Daisy Mae. Believe me when I tell you that she should have been named Crazy Daisy. She's pretty hyper, even by my standards, but she can also be very sweet. Some friends have since adopted her and moved her to the country.

Hah! But she will never replace my original girlfriend. While I lived in Florida, my heart was always a flutter when Miss Cricket walked past my house. That fluffy little Border Collie is still unrivaled!

I also have some very good human friends that I had to leave behind in Florida. Bob really loves me. The same goes for Tom, Beth, Frank, Gloria, Myrna, and just plain everyone who ever met me. The night before I left, Gloria came to visit and brought me a new little red and white teddy bear toy.

Needless to say, I love it and promptly showed her that she'd "done good" by grabbing hold of the little bear and thrashing it all about! I also made my rather famous sound that I call my "play growl." That made her laugh at my viciousness!!!

Then, when she and Frank stood across the street, I demonstrated my lightning speed one more time. I raced full tilt to their open arms. They love watching me barrel down the road… a streak of flying fur, so to speak.

On my last morning in Florida, I also paid a visit to Tom and Beth. They had put a special seat for me in front of one of their windows. That helped me to watch the birds in their back yard. And the golfers, who I understand were trying for some birdies of their own. Tom and Beth are super.

They say they will adopt me if I can't adapt to life in New Hampshire. I mean, you know how it is. I'm a native Floridian. (Yes, there really are some of those!) I am not sure what will happen when I see things like snow! So far, I think they just make it up for TV and movies.

Humans are funny. Even when they've known us for a long time, they can forget basic things… like our NAMES! Really. Humans often forget my name is Bandit. They call me "So Cute" all the time! I hear it's a training issue, so I don't really mind. They can call me whatever they like; it's okay.

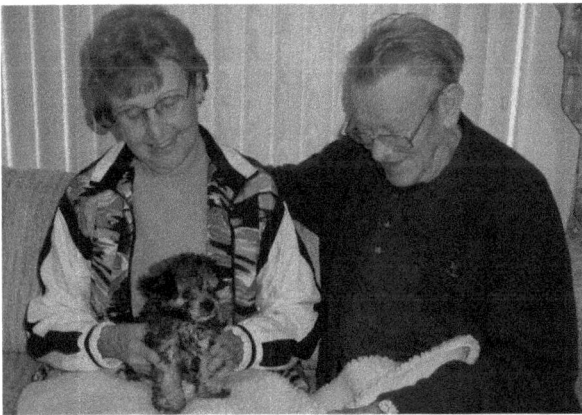

My first day in my first home in Florida,
with my Aunt Phyllis & Uncle Bob Leggett visiting me

Life is full of changes. Changes teach me to appreciate every day, every little leaf that tries to flutter past me, and each tiny morsel of my crunchies. I used to take these things for granted. Now I am devoted to getting better and better at hanging loose and taking it all in my stride. AND teaching my humans to do the same.

You can do it, too. Get ready now, as I start serving up lots more incredible tips and secrets for getting and keeping your humans in line! Truly… No leashes required.

3

TRAINING THE TRAINER

While we warn against letting this book fall into the hands of humans, we do encourage you to pass on all great tips you learn from this book or any other source to every other canine you know. The more of us we get trained, the faster we'll get the humans on this planet on track.

So, we are not just students when it comes to learning the best and fastest ways to help our humans. We are also training other dogs to be trainers to help their humans, too.

I've even heard humans say this same thing. "Dogs are easy to train. It's humans that pose the biggest challenge." So, even some humans understand that they can be tricky.

We must be patient and persistent. THAT, my friends, will be a repeating theme in this book, I'm afraid.

Keep in mind that we can't control others. We can teach and set an example, but we also need to recognize that not everyone wants to live as we do. Sometimes we must learn to simply celebrate the uniqueness of others. I mean, we all look different. So, it's not so peculiar that we all think and behave differently also.

Humans always seem to be trying to BE "different." Yet sometimes they can overdo it. We must help them see the perfect glee we can all get from being part of the pack. That does not mean that we don't recognize and enjoy our individuality.

Value your uniqueness to avoid being too tough on yourself…
especially when the training isn't going so well.

Ah, yes… my first hoodie

There will be times when our humans just don't seem to "get it." Perfection would actually be boring. (I heard there was some old book or movie about that theme… It was called something like "The Stepford Dogs.")

Okay, let me get back on point here. You see, I went through a health challenge that got the humans all kinds of scared. In the end, my doctor had to cut a big cyst off one side of my lower lip, which actually left a notch missing.

Hah! It's another part of my uniqueness now. Humans tend to get upset over these things. I laughed, seeee, and tried to explain that the doc was simply giving me a place to hold my cigar when I do my Edward G. Robinson gangster impersonation, seeee! Hah!

Anyway, part of training the trainer is encouraging every dog (and human) we know to go gleefully through life, celebrating both our uniqueness AND being part of the pack.

Speaking of your pack, remember to let each and every member know that they are very special to you. For example, my pack includes my Keira human. My folks say she's the number one oldest daughter, but she is my Keira.

Though she doesn't live with us any longer, she is still part of my pack. (Once you're mine, Babe, you stay mine! That's one of my Bandit rules.)

With my Keira

I keep trying to take a photograph of her, because she is so pretty, but she can be a little bit shy sometimes. I will keep working on it.

Sometimes I visit with Keira and James at their place. They have taken me on lots of fun adventures, like hiking and mountain climbing. (Okay, okay... They sometimes carry me.) But I still have to remind them that they are totally part of my pack... each and every time they visit.

This includes rushing to the door and leaping gleefully. It also means spending a wee bit of time giving my Keira a refresher course in some of her training successes. So, I start by letting her rub my belly. Then we must play a rousing game of Chase Me, Chase Me.

I also like to take her through a few other basics, such as polishing up her High 5 skills. Yup! She remembers both high (uptown) and low (downtown) variations.

When she does really well, I even let her give me a cookie, but I always let her cuddle me, play with me, and tell me how wonderful I am.

4

BASIC TRAINING COMPONENTS 🐾

Obedience -- Getting your human to come
- Roll on your back; they will come to rub your belly.

- Pick a spot to stare at and growl, as if you see a ghost.

- Okay, you can always do one of the things they hate. For example, scratch their floor, rug or a piece of furniture.

Consistency
- If you are truly desperate, and the training isn't going well, you can always barf. Throwing up gets them to come to you so fast you won't believe it. However, they tend to not be happy with that, so you don't want to try this except in dire circumstances.

Skills

- Pull on your leash.

    o Leashes help humans to not get lost.

    o Without training, they only walk in straight lines. They need guidance to zigzag and not miss out on all the special sights and smells that we can show them.

    o Pulling them on a leash also keeps them walking more briskly, which is very important to help protect your human from turning into a coach potato.

- Wear sunglasses. We all must protect our eyes from the bright sunlight. If you wear yours, they are more apt to remember to wear theirs, too.

- Slow down... a little. Remember that your human doesn't have four legs, so they can't always keep up. However, they need to run or at least trot... It's good exercise for them and fun for us!

- Chew things. Sure, we'd be thrilled with toys of our own, but THEIR shoes, books, socks, pillows, towels, or whatever will always do in a pinch. If they give you your own toys and praise you for playing with them, rather than their things, okay. Stick to your toys. This also trains them to get you even more toys! However, if they don't praise you for avoiding their toys, be persistent. Play with anything you want; you win either way! Remember, they'd rather praise us than scold us, so I like to give them as many opportunities to praise me as possible.

- Jump on people. Very little gets humans more excited than this, especially when we've just come inside from rain or snow. If you want to see them get super animated, give this a go! This can also help them to dance. Demonstrate on your own by jumping around just on your back two legs. This better imitates the way they stand and need to move to dance. Just remember, it's even more fun when you do it _with_ your human.

Socialization
- As much as we love them, our humans are still basically animals. We need to work with them to help them be their best.

- Humans need protecting; always alert them to squirrels, horses or cows, squirrels, deer, turkeys, and especially squirrels. (Uh, did I mention squirrels?)

- Be patient. Not all humans are really good at getting acquainted with their environment.

- Show them the importance of sniffing out every single creature, large and small. Don't skip smelling leaves, flowers, or mud puddles either.

Studying a lizard on the window sill

- Exude positive energy. Don't get sad or anxious or frustrated when your humans struggle to learn. They tend to get sad and frustrated and overworked and moody and so much more.

- One of our biggest responsibilities is to show them the importance of putting on a happy snout.

Leadership
- Train your human to be the Alpha Dog, Leader of the Pack, Big Kahuna, A #1.

    o They want this role, but it doesn't always come naturally. They actually will typically let us run all over them.

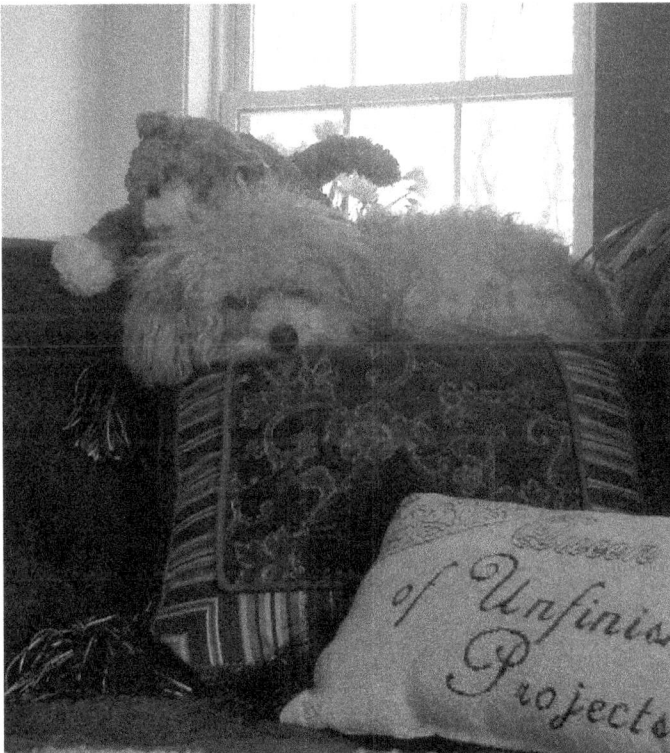

o We are packers... we love being part of a pack. We hate it when any member of our pack is missing... even for a few minutes. But every pack needs a leader, or we'll just sleep all day or something silly.

o No bullying; we like being lovers way more than being fighters. However, some humans have trouble with this. They can get a warped concept that pushing others around makes them bigger and more respected. Oops! The opposite is true. Pushing others around and being a bully makes us smaller and less respected. Be patient with your human if they struggle with this. They are, after all, merely human.

o End each day with a kiss...

Feeding Time – Humans are not always good at schedules.

- Stare at them while they eat or prepare food.
- How to get goodies from the table:

- o Beg… adorably.

- o Stare (if begging isn't allowed).

- o Remember, if they toss you a scrap from the table once, you've GOT 'Em! They <u>will</u> do it again.

- o Miss no opportunity to look longingly at guests! Company seems to train on this skill more quickly than our own humans. Go figure.

Time to go "Out"
- If you have a cat, they can help by yowling. They love a good reason to sing.

- Grab your leash and take it to them… repeatedly, if need be.

Speaking

- If the human says, "No," start by ignoring them. Keep barking. Now comes the important part. If the human does nothing, Bingo! "No" means "Yes!" Humans, it turns out, don't re-train easily. Obviously, they needed to try something different, but they get comfortable.

Problem Solving – Troubleshooting
- Never say critical things like, "Bad human."

- Remember to be patient. Training your human takes time.

- Settle down. We like to be frisky.

On the boat with Adam, Caiti & Franklin

5

NAME GAME & LINGO BINGO

Remembering your name isn't always easy for humans. As I mentioned earlier, since I was born, I have been called "So Cute." Naturally, when my humans named me Bandit, other humans struggled to get it right. They were told my name is Bandit, but they'd continually "Ooh" and "Ah" and say, "He's so cute!" To this day very little has changed. It's probably much the same for you.

Then and now

Even my own humans confuse easily. They and their friends keep calling me all sorts of names in addition to Bandit. Seriously.

The list grows: El Bandito, Little Hugger Bugger, Lamb Chops, Wonder Child, FlufferNutter, Love Bug, Ragamuffin, Puppy, Sweet Pea, Dogzilla, Little Monkey, Bandie Boy, and on and on.

Often, they call me Twinkle Toes. I think this is because they call my humongous cat Thunder Hooves when he gallops up or down the stairs... because I am more light-footed. My friend, Paul... the one they call Sully... came up with one of the best names for me. He calls me Mr. Wiggles because I wiggle like crazy whenever someone comes to visit me. My humans insist these are just nicknames, but I think they say that so I won't think that I have failed to train them to remember my name.

My humans have trouble with my kitty's name, too. My Ronald human loves the Yankees baseball team, so he named the kitty, Jeeter, after a star player, Derek Jeter. However, my Cathy human is a Red Sox fan, so she didn't want a Yankee in the house. She agreed with the name by adding an extra letter "e" in the first syllable. See, humans are silly. Even though they agreed on his name, they still call Jeeter all sorts of things. I already told you he gets called Thunder Hooves. They also call him Cat, Purr Monger, Furmeister, Fat Cat, Fuzzy Face, Furball, Meow Meow, and The Kraken.

Here's the deal. When it comes to some skills, it's better to just let the humans do the best they can. They mean well. Don't drive yourself crazy. They can learn some words, however. For example, among the words my humans have

learned are:	No	Come	Out
Yard	Bandit	Big Yard	Little Yard
Paws Up	Up	Down	Wave
Sit	We're busy	Lay Down	Roll Over
Bang	Shake	Other Paw	Squirrel
High Five	Up Town	Low Five	Down Town
Dog	Truck	Dance	Cookie
Rabbit	Duck	Kitty	Jeeter
Bring it	Get it	Drop it	Not yours
No speak	Shhhhh	Indoor voice	Huggy Buggy
No growl	No bite	Chase me!	Go for a ride
Breakfast	Supper	Crunchies	Go around
In your bag	Bed	That's just TV	Night Night

These words were easy, but humans struggle to learn even basic lingo. For example, when I hear a car pull up to our house, I make a simple and plain announcement before the people even get out of their car. I say, "Hey! Full alert! Someone's here! Everybody to the front door! Now!" My humans hear, "Woof! Woof woof! Woof woof woof woof woof! Woof!" Seriously?

Oh, well. Did you ever hear advice like, "Don't try to teach a pig to sing"? There's a good reason for such sage wisdom. You would just frustrate yourself and annoy the pig. Keep this in mind when it comes to a human remembering basic lingo and even your name.

Here's my best Bandit advice: Let your humans call you anything they like... as long as they don't call you late to dinner!

6

KINDNESS COUNTS

A very important lesson we can teach our humans involves kindness. Our differences don't matter. Be kind to others. It sounds rather obvious, but we have to keep reminding our humans sometimes. You never see a dog trying to achieve happiness by destroying happiness in others. Even if our human has done something that is not right, we are still kind to them.

THIS is a great example to set for them. Being kind is far more important than being right. We must help them keep perspective. It's not always about "you." Humans definitely forget that sometimes.

My own towel after a swim

We also set the tone by never mocking or making fun of anyone, especially not the way they talk, or laugh, or dance, or eat, or dress, or anything! We surely wouldn't want our humans to get intimidated and not dare do any of those things in front of us. Think of the fun we'd miss out on if we did. Yet, our humans poke fun at their friends' expense sometimes… okay, it seems to happen frequently. Keep showing them that we would never do such unkind things to them or anyone else. It's unnatural.

It's actually natural to be kind. As we set the example day after day, they'll see it's the small, simple kindnesses that impact others so profoundly. They need to practice daily. We help by cheering for them, jumping with glee, or just wagging our tails like crazy each and every time they do any and every little kindness.

You know… putting fresh water in our bowl, walking with us, patting our heads, "scritching" under our chins, rubbing our ears, tossing a stick or ball, playing a little tug-of-war game, or giving us an extra cookie. Let no opportunity pass you by. Curl up with them or stand by their side… wherever they may be.

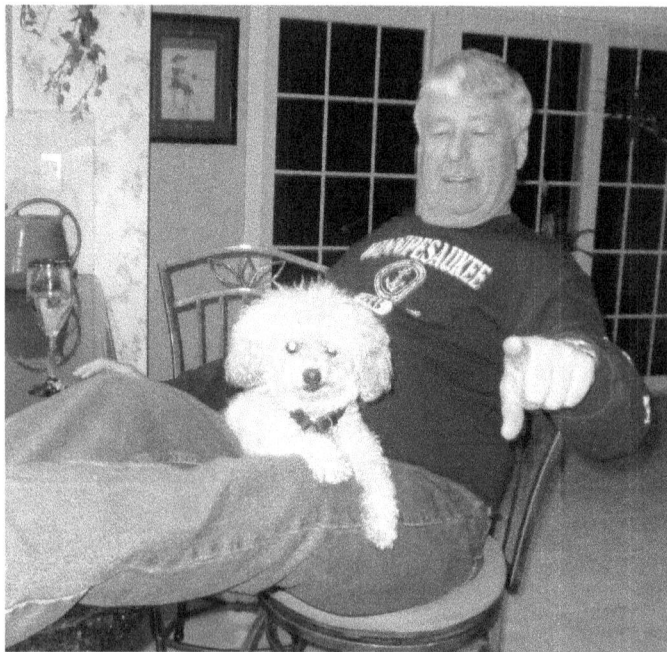

Hanging out with The Ronald

7

GETTING TO KNOW YOU – PURRRFECT BUDDIES

Reading things your humans write about you is a great way to get to know what makes them tick. Just don't let them know that you can read their "lingo," or they might try to hide such delights or bury them in the back yard.

I must tell you that I found the weirdest note, written by my Cathy human. She sent it to my original Poppy and Mom a month after I moved in.

Before I share the missive with you, let me explain that I had never before met this thing called a cat. Jeeter is my first. I understand that this particular cat is no typical 10-pound feline. Oh, no. He weighs in at 18 pounds! (Sheeez! I only top out at 7 pounds.) He is not _round_ in shape, but he is _huge_!

So, they say that he and my first dog buddy got along beautifully before I moved here. Hmmmm.... But Jeeter was dramatically smaller than the Newfie. And Jeeter is dramatically larger than I am, though I hate to admit any such thing. So, when I first arrived, I was surprised that this kitty was so intimidated by me. I guess it was just odd for him to meet a Maltipoo.

So, here is the note my Cathy human wrote to bring my folks up to date on my carrying on with the Jeeter kitty.

"We are pleased to report that Bandit and Jeeter are officially buddies now! Jeeter suddenly started approaching with less fear. They went nose to nose several times. Jeeter even started "bumping" his forehead on Bandit as he does to our faces. They now get along beautifully. Of course, when El Bandito gets toooo rambunctious, Jeeter recoils a bit. But it only took a couple swats from him to straighten Bandit out. It is very cute to watch them together.

Thankfully, when fluffy I "look" much larger!

Jeeter does this thing with us where he "hides" and crouches in his ready-to-spring stance. As we pass by, he pounces out and wraps his front paws around one of our ankles. He just did it with Bandit this morning. Then they spent a few minutes chasing each other around the back yard. It was AWESOME!

Oh, both sleep upstairs with us now. Bandit ends up going to his crate after they've played for a while. Jeeter starts out on the bed, but tends to end up in the bathroom on the bath mat near his new buddy.

How's that for an amazing turnaround?"

Jeeter, with Poppy's phone and my duck

See the cool stuff we can learn by reading what the humans write. I now do this all the time.

Okay, so now you have it. I am not sure this is a cool thing… getting along with a cat and all that. But over the years I do admit that Jeeter and I have become the best of pals. We sometimes tease The Ronald human by using his remote control to change the TV channels. Then we both put on our best "innocent" faces. Hee Hee! I've even caught my kitty playing with one of my stuffed ducks AND trying to make a call on Poppy's cell phone.

So, share with your humans my advice on helping critters adjust to other critters in your home. Just give us some love and some time together. We will work it out.

Now Jeeter and I must get back to watching one of our favorite TV shows... It's close between "Castle" and "Law and Order."

8

THE BASIC BELLY RUB

Start simply with your humans. The basic belly rub is an absolute "must" for all humans to learn. They catch on to this skill very quickly, so it's a great starting point.

Humans tend to have fragile egos, so it's important to start them with a skill at which they can easily succeed. This builds their confidence. And we pooches get the value-added benefit of getting our bellies rubbed... frequently! Who can argue with that?!?

Now, even if your humans don't get it right in the very first session, don't stop there. I recommend repeating this simple essential at least once daily.

Once you get good at inspiring a belly rub on your first attempt with some humans, you've hit the Belly Rub Bonanza. Simply train every human you meet to do this. I'm not kidding. This works like a charm.

I don't care who comes to call. I get immediate success with everyone, from the UPS driver to the heating repair man, from my humans' favorite computer geek to the flower delivery driver. I even enjoy consistent success with humans who claim to not like dogs at all... and they even grin about it and say they liked doing it! Hey, trust me; I'm a dog. If I can do it, you can too!

Best Bandit Step-by-Step:

#1   Say a happy, nice-to-see-you, "Woof!"

#2   Immediately lay down and roll onto your back.

That's it. What could be easier? But here's the secret: After you've bared your belly, don't move. This is key. No more wiggling, jumping, woofing, or anything else.

Whoever makes the next move loses. And whoever stays still, wins. Win that belly rub!

This is especially effective with little children or anyone who might think they are afraid of dogs. I mean, when we are on our backs, grinning at them, we are at their mercy. There can be no doubt about our good intensions. We are certainly not in a biting or growling or otherwise menacing pose.

Oh, and this belly rubbing exercise also makes humans smile and laugh, especially when they watch how easily I train brand new humans who arrive on the scene. My humans always say the same thing, "That's our Bandit… seven pounds of fun, fur and fury."

Hah! My cover is safe. My disguise is holding. Folks don't even suspect that I'm a 150-pound Newfie underneath my Maltipoo exterior!

9

COOKIES

Some experts insist that we should never train our humans by rewarding them with goodies. I disagree. The way to your human's heart is through their stomach... er, uh, <u>our</u> stomachs.

Training can be a thankless task. But, sometimes when they do well, the humans will give you a cookie.

Sometimes they even give us extra cookies. I use these to teach them to decorate. Stash tidbits of treats or biscuits or bones or extra cookies wherever possible. I like putting them in potted plants and trees, behind pillows on the sofas and chairs, and even in the bottom of my toy box. Keep doing this. They may catch on and start decorating with dog cookies all on their own.

Bark and complain to get what you want. We are not doing this with selfish motivation. Oh, no! This is an important skill for humans. They do things like go out to restaurants for dinner. If someone fails to deliver properly, your humans need to know to bark!

Swim time with Dad

Remember to pay attention to what you humans are doing. For example, it's super easy to score treats when they are cooking. Simply stand directly behind them... very quietly. Then, when they back up and almost fall over you, they are apt to spill a goody or two while they catch their balance.

Regardless, they will know very quickly that giving you a treat will get you out of their way. Hee hee hee! We get the goodies! It's always Treat Time!

10

SHARE ENTHUSIASTICALLY

Hugs are one of our most effective training tools. Positive reinforcement. Let them know they are good humans, even when they are frustrating… as humans can be. Hug them and kiss them; nuzzle your snout into their neck. My humans now even say, "Huggie Buggie" when they want a hug. I deliver. Sometimes they say it over and over and over… I just keep on hugging and nuzzling.

Snuggle in with them whenever possible. Express yourself. Show them love. They will catch on and actually look forward to your attention. Hah! We will work for treats… and hugs. Humans also respond to snuggling. How nice. This is truly a Win-Win!

I've even gotten The Ronald human to let me help captain his boat. Now THAT's a really cool treat!

Humans need a lot of reinforcement... loving, gentle encouragement. They get nerved up over "stuff." We canines know to avoid people in sour moods. We don't want grumpiness to rub off on us. But humans get confused. They think they can change someone's thinking and bad moods. Nope. Sour humans must change themselves. The best we can do is offer comfort. Anyone putting up with a crabby person reeeeally needs that comfort. Everything is better with a friend.

So, stay cool and calm, seemingly without a care. They'll say things like, "It's a dog's life." That's a true indication that you're doing great, because we've got them convinced that being a dog equates with living without a care in the world. Well, okay. We don't worry about world peace or climate change, but we do worry! We worry a lot. For example, we wonder about really important things, like when we'll get the next cookie or belly rub.

I prefer to leave the planetary issues for those silly humans who think politics will take care of everything.

In truth, loving touch is very healing. Rub against your human whenever possible. Snuggle up. Help them feel the love. This sets the right example for humans, which is a great way to train them to offer loving touch more often.

TV time with Dad

11

SQUIRREL PLEASE

We all have a favorite toy. Mine is my stuffed Squirrel. It's really my Teddy Bear, and I sleep with it every night.

I don't know about your humans, but mine think it's clever to ration my time with my Squirrel. So, they take it away every morning and put it up high out of my reach.

You see, it's very important to train your humans to give you your favorite things. They do tend to forget.

For example, in the evening when I want my Teddy Bear... er...ah... Squirrel, I had to come up with a way to be sure they give it to me. I taught them that if they say, "Night Night" to me, I will dutifully trot straight into my kennel crate and lie down. They then give me my Squirrel. Cool.

Sometimes I'd surprise them. If they forgot to close the door right away, I'd grab my Squirrel in my mouth and zoom out of my crate. Ha! Then they'd have to play a little hide-and-seek or tug-of-war before bedtime. Humans love this. Just try it a few times. Yours will catch on fast, too.

Now, when I got my second humans, I must admit that they were a little slower on the uptake than my first ones. They sometimes totally forgot to give me my Squirrel and tuck me into bed. Seriously.

In cases like this you need to come up with a way to alert them and get them thinking straight again. For my first hint, I lie down in my crate with my front half totally sticking out so they can see me. Sigh. Nada. Bupkis.

They usually don't notice this. So, I have to kick it up a notch.

My second hint is to stand in front of the crate and stare at them. Nope, they're not apt to notice this hint either.

Proceed to Hint #3 for certain success. Using your left front paw, deftly hook the edge of your crate's door and I wing it open. Immediately after that, switch to your right front paw and slam the door closed with a Bang! Immediately look at your humans to assess whether or not it worked. If they aren't moving toward you, simply repeat the door slamming again. (Oh, reverse which paw you use for each action, if your crate door opens the opposite direction.)

I continue this process until light dawns on marble head. Sure enough, they start laughing, get up and get my Squirrel. I then sit politely until they say, "Night Night." I then dutifully scamper into my crate, turn around, and receive my Squirrel.

Be patient with your humans. They get it, but they often forget it. Opening and slamming your crate door repeatedly will get their attention and remind them.

Just pick one special thing that it should mean to them to help avoid confusion. Remember, and I must repeat myself... They are mere humans, after all.

Give it a try. Wing your crate door open. Slam it shut. Bang! Look at them. Wing it open. Slam it shut. Bang! Look at them again. Repeat as many times as needed to reinforce the skill you're training then to do.

Try this. You'll love it. So will your humans!

My crate always fascinates my kitty.

12

ZZZZZZZZ's

If you really want your humans to be more trainable, start with encouraging them to sleep longer and take frequent naps. Humans have this weird habit of setting alarm clocks. Figure out how to shut it off and do so when they are not looking. Do whatever it takes to keep them in bed longer each morning. Hey, it's good for their health! You're only thinking of them.

Encouraging my Aunt June to stop reading

Napping is also one of the great pleasures of each and every day. I hate sleeping through my morning nap. Hee hee!

One of my favorite nap spots is a sunspot. They form all over the house at different times of day. I don't even need a pillow when I land in one of those. It's so warm and toasty. Just curl up and snooze.

This act looks (and is) so comfortable and soothing that it automatically draws your human in with you. I have not found that they especially like to curl up in sunspots, but it does get them thinking about having a nap.

Naturally, each time my human stretches out on the bed, I shift gears immediately. I will even leave my favorite sunspot to curl up with my human. My Ronald human has learned to nap beautifully. He stretches out on the bed and turns on the TV. It's usually some DIY home makeover show or a "Law and Order" rerun. I don't care. I can sleep through any show.

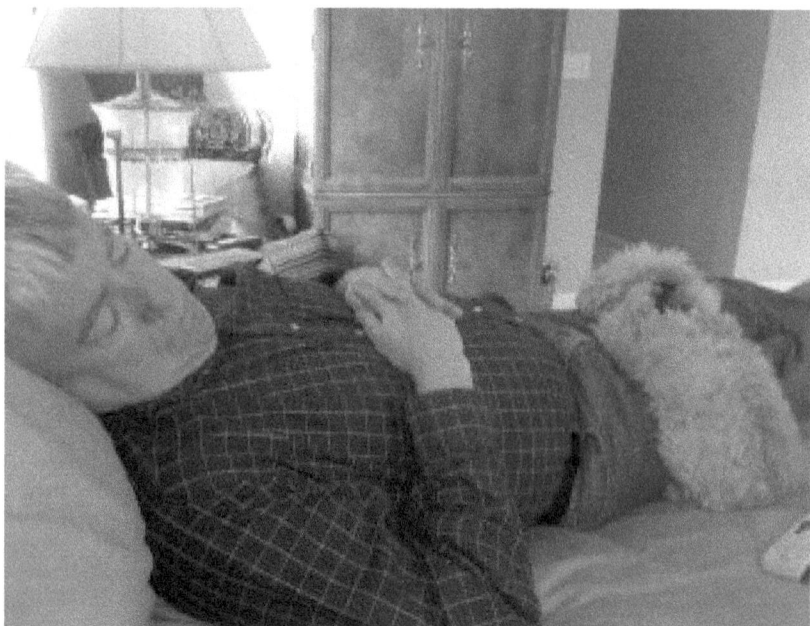

Except when car doors slam or sirens blare or doorbells ring. You know. Then my humans have to remind me, "It's only TV." Sigh. I always think someone has come to visit me. Cookies and friends are both worthy reasons to interrupt a great nap.

A perfect way to train your human to stay napping is to climb up on top of them and stretch out, so they cannot move. Then close your eyes and pretend you are sleeping, even when you are not.

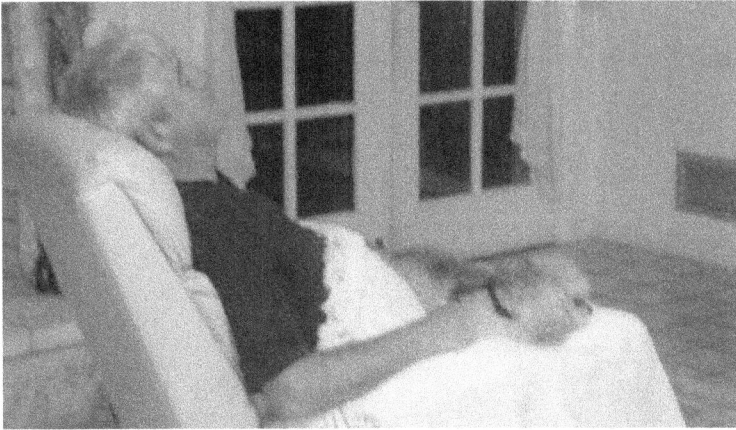

This makes them feel guilty if they disturb you. Hee hee! I love it. Usually, they just nod off, which means that I can, too.

This works. The Ronald human has this down pat! He has become a World Class napper... thanks to me! You can make this work for your human also.

Seriously, teaching your human to nap is very important. Naps improve alertness, boost memory, improve performance, and help them feel rejuvenated. That means they will have more energy for playing! Win-win!

13

FOOD, GLORIOUS FOOD 🐾

This nose knows when a cookie is trying to hide!

Never let food go to waste. Oh, wait! I am so barking at... er, uh, preaching to the choir here. I do think that this is a lesson we need to teach to humans. Wasting food is bad.

In the United States alone, I have heard it said that 30% of all food is thrown away every year. Even half that amount is too much. Man, I would never let such yumminess go to waste.

Sometimes our humans don't mean to waste food, but they do tend to drop food on the floor while preparing meals and even while dining. Personally, I cannot imagine dropping even one morsel of chow and not immediately scooping it right back up. One of our sworn canine responsibilities is cleaning up after our humans' little spills, after all... along with watering hydrants and trees, of course.

Oh, and my kitty is a very messy eater. The humans put his food dish up high so I can't reach it (drat), but I will stretch to great lengths to clean up his spillage!

I also try to set the right example for my humans by really getting into my food. Literally. I have been known to be so excited about my approaching food dish that I scamper straight through my water dish.

All the while, I hear my Cathy human singing a silly song from the Broadway musical, "You're a Good Man, Charlie Brown." "Oh, it's Suppertime! Yeah, it's Suppertime! Supp-Supp-Suppertime, very best time of day. Wintertime's nice with the ice and snow. Summertime's nice with a place to go. Bedtime. Overtime. Halftime, too. But they just can't hold a candle to my Suppertime! Oh, yeahhhhhh!" Seriously. That's fun; she really gets into getting my food ready. But just give me my filled food dish for cryin' out loud.

Actually, I do appreciate anyone who shares my complete and total enthusiasm for food! And I kinda like it when she sings to me. Don't tell her that though. I like her to think she needs to keep practicing.

I do not like to share my treats or my supper. I will share love all day long. My goodies are strictly off-limits.

That's not to say that I can't compromise in emergencies. Cooperation can be vital. A special food lesson for our humans can be found in the spirit of cooperation. We are pretty good at this, though our humans don't necessarily know it. Sometimes we actually keep this skill hidden from our humans, so they feel needed. But, in truth, it sure comes in handy.

A good example comes from a little stunt I pulled off with my friend Maggie Mae. She and her humans came to visit me. After they gave us our supper, the humans went out to dinner. Ha-ha-ha! They left a big plastic bag of Maggie's crunchies on the kitchen counter.

Maggie Mae

Okay, did I mention I only weigh 7 pounds? Maggie's a bit bigger, coming in around 25 pounds. Neither of us is very tall... certainly not tall enough to snag that big bag of goodies off the counter. But we are dogs. We are invincible!

Maggie wasn't all that interested in her food to begin with, and she didn't particularly want to help me score some extras. But we dogs do know cooperation. So, we set about to get the goodies.

We tried leaping as high as possible. Nope. We tried stretching and trying to latch onto the bag with our teeth. Nada. We even tried to push a chair closer to the kitchen. Nothin' doin'.

Man, oh, man. Time is of the essence here. They'll only be gone for a while. Desperate times call for desperate measures.

Don't tell our humans how we did this. I know we can trust you.

Maggie stood right beside the counter. She let me leap onto her back. Nowwwww I could stand on my back legs and almost get my teeth onto the corner of that bag. If I can just stretch a little bit more…. Nope. I had to give one little jump. The poodle part of me can really leap, so this worked beautifully.

Of course, once I had grabbed the baggie, I failed to land safely back on Maggie's back. I mean, I sort of did, but then I immediately slid down her side and crash-landed on the floor. Hey! That's a very small price to pay for a very big score!

I easily ripped into the plastic bag, and the goodies tumbled all over the floor. Yabba-dabba-doo! Mags was such a lady. She delicately ate a couple of pieces. I think she was just joining me to be polite, because she said she really wasn't hungry. I proceeded to gobble up the entire contents.

The humans were quite distraught, by the bulging size of my belly. (I think they considered changing my name to Fat Albert that night.)

They had more food in the cupboard, but I have to be honest with you. I had zero interest in even one more bite of food for two full days. That's ultra-rare for me! Burp!

14

CLEAN UP: AISLE 5

I've never been in one of the humans' supermarkets, but I understand a voice comes on a loudspeaker if someone spills something. "Clean Up: Aisle 5!" Then someone comes running to get the mess off the floor. They have to do this so no customer will slip and fall.

We canines also take this responsibility very seriously. If something falls on the floor, we feel obligated to scurry to the scene of the crime and scarf it up... fast. This is just so that no one slips and falls, mind you.

This is one of those opportunities to benefit personally by training our humans to try something they've probably heard before anyway. Encourage them to use the line, "Clean Up: Aisle 5" at home... in the unlikely event that we failed to see that some wonderful morsel has fallen to the floor. This works very well at my house, and it can in yours, too.

Naturally, I still encourage my fellow canines to continue the usual perimeter and floor checks, especially when the humans are cooking, grilling, or dining. Having them always announce any spillage, however, guarantees we won't miss a treat... I mean a beat.

This is purely logical. I could be taking a nap or be playing with my cat. I might not be in the room to see that they dropped something. Well, now they don't have to bend down to pick up any food item. They simply call out, "Clean Up: Aisle 5." I come scurrying.

If your humans have gotten too tidy lately, which means they have been shirking their duty to drop a morsel somewhere for you, immediate action is required! Put on your very best sad face. Hold in your belly if you must. But the ultra-forlorn, woe-is-me expression is paramount!

If you need a little coaching on the putting on a super-sad face, okay. You are about to have one of those "ah-hah" moments. We've all seen the television commercials seeking support for our fellow dogs who are in distress. They sit in their crates and look through the bars at the cameras. I mean, who can resist?

"For just 18-dollars a month you could feed this poor, starving dog. Your donation today will make sure these animals no longer go hungry." It may sound rather "snarky" of me, but I have seen the commercial enough that even I tried to dial in and save a dog. But I had to settle for wearing their sad expression and batting my big, round eyes whenever I feel my humans have missed an opportunity to give me a treat. Whew, I am one lucky dog!

15

WALK THE HUMAN 🐾

One of the toughest things for a human to learn is that Life is more about the journey, and not just the destination. All they have to do is take a breath and watch us... we zig zag as we stroll, so as to not miss any delight that might be along the way. We enjoy every single moment. We take it all in every day, even if we just walked the exact same route two hours earlier.

Sometimes there's a big yard or even a meadow where our humans let us romp and play. Sometimes there is pavement or concrete and not a blade of grass to be seen. It matters little to us.

While we enjoy playing in groups or by ourselves, what matters most is to have our humans with us as much as possible. Humans, however, tend to get and keep themselves very busy. For them, all too often, walking us only has to do with us doing our business. It's vital for us dogs to train them otherwise.

Whether they require a leash or not, walk your human regularly. This is good for them physically, mentally, and emotionally. We are helping them be stronger, smarter, and happier humans!

Keep your humans moving. This not only reduces stress, but it decreases depression. I only know this from hearing about it. As a dog, I haven't the slightest clue how to be depressed. Dogs are too busy being happy to be alive.

Humans seem to become aware that health is their most valuable asset many years into their lives. They usually have squandered their puppy years and suddenly find themselves struck with conditions like substance abuse or addictions, heart disease, diabetes, and cancers. If we teach them about health earlier, we might help them avoid some of the common health pitfalls.

I am a huge advocate of drinking lots of water, exercising often, eating my food, napping frequently, and playing almost all the rest of the time. THAT's my Success Formula!

If we can get our humans to do just those few things, they will be healthier and happier.

Remember, age is just a number. There are so many charts and graphs that say how old we canines are in human years. If only our humans could understand that they are way older than they need to be at almost any age.

Sigh. Again, set the example for your humans. Stay a puppy just as long as your body permits it. When the body goes, keep that puppy spirit. Be forever young at heart. Getting old, unfortunately, is mandatory. Growing up is optional. Opt out.

Give me a big "woof" for THAT one. WOOF!

16

LET ME IN; LET ME OUT

I admit that I have heard it said that dogs are always on the wrong side of the door… or window. Okay, it's true.

Sometimes, that is simply one way of keeping our humans moving. Let us in. Let us out. Let us in. Let us out. It's as natural as breathing.

I happen to know that humans tend to think that the grass is always greener on the other side of the door, but that is not the case with us canines. We just haven't figured out how to be inside and outside at the same time.

Before I forget, let me tell you one silly story about a door. I was about 5 years old. My humans followed me dutifully to the sliding glass door that I like to take to go out to the deck and back yard.

I started to gallop through the open door, but shockeroo! A wall of white icy crystals towered high above my head!

I heard my Cathy human laughing. She had a shovel ready. As I backed away from this weird blockade, she started scooping huge mounds of this white fluffy stuff off to the side. Soon I had a trail to walk through. She continued shoveling a path straight out onto the lawn for me.

Yup, I met this snow stuff. It is NOT just some marketing ploy or Hollywood set. It's for real. And it is cold!

When snow gets really deep The Ronald human uses his big snow blowing machine to make giant paths for me!

Man, that's nice, but the ground beneath my toes still gets pretty darn chilly! Never mind how it felt to plant my cheeks on this silly snow stuff to do my business. Yikes! I'd been told about snow, but I really thought my buddies were just making it up, like folklore... old doggie's tales.

I don't care how much my kitty, Jeeter, tries to show me how "fun" snow is, I think he's got brain freeze. Well, he spent his first couple years out on the streets before my humans adopted him, so I guess it's natural for him.

But I'm a Floridian, for barkin' out loud!

Anyway, doors are meant to be walked through. Getting outside becomes especially important when our humans have left the building. Duh!

But it's also important when someone is arriving, like someone delivering the mail or a package, or just some friend showing up. We like to get out there and take charge of what's going on, not to mention barking a full alert that someone has arrived.

We also love running to doors when our humans return from anywhere. When a door opens, we want to be first through each and every door. This is very important for dogs. We teach our humans this fact by doing it each and every time.

Open the door, please!

Humans sometimes wonder why we seem to have a hankering to go outside when they had us outside an hour earlier. Silly humans.

It's to get them to do something with us, that's all. Thinking that we might really need to go outside to do some business gets them to take us out again… and again.

When the humans are lazy, they merely "let" us out. It's way more fun when they go with us. So, we will wait a little while, and give them the open-the-door cues again… and again… and again.

Bandit & Jeeter

Jeeter and Miles

17

CARRY ME! CARRY ME! OR NOT

Misty is an absolutely gorgeous Sheltie. She's all kinds of fluffy. Most importantly, she figured out some amazing skills early in her life. As a result, she is the epitome of princess. She wouldn't have it any other way.

Princess Misty, another Furrever Dog

For example, she has her very own room at her house. In the middle stands the most amazing mountain of toys I have ever seen. If someone makes a toy, she has it.

Also, she only eats organic food, prepared fresh for her daily. Rumor has it that she dines from crystal bowls and is served her meals by another princess. Wow!

When she goes for a walk, her humans use only a pink leash and matching, color-coordinated bags for picking up "big business." Here's the best part, they literally carry her over any rough surfaces, such as crushed stones.

Now THAT is a skill we should all teach our humans. Let's learn from Misty.

Keep in mind, when most of us go for a walk, it's more simplistic. Our humans may open a door and let us zoom. Or, if they might get lost or something, you can walk with them, but keep them holding onto their leash.

If you'd like to teach them the "Carry Me" technique, try a couple easy tips. If you are walking on a nice surface, such as grass, simply stop in your tracks when it changes to something "ouchy" like crushed rock or "icky" like a giant mud puddle. When they try to encourage you to continue, cower back. Quiver with "fear" if you can do it. If they persist or even give some command to continue, you may have to resort to an audible whimper. Do what you must, but hold your ground. They will pick you up and carry you across the "ouchy" surface.

Once they've accomplished this skill just once or twice, they will have it down. You, too, will be carried like Princess Misty.

On the other hand, if you are a huge dog, or if you really like "ouchy" or "icky" surfaces, like I do, you need to apply some opposite techniques.

First of all, humans can't lift us up if we weigh a lot, especially if we weigh more than they do. Hee hee. I have some buddies like that.

For most of us, however, we need to be very clever to get to explore all the various surfaces that we find so interesting. Train your humans to think that they are getting *their* way, when they are actually doing exactly what we want. You may notice that this upcoming lesson is a sort of recurring theme for me. Humans need LOTS of work here.

I do this all the time by employing one simple technique. Let's say that I've been out in the back yard. Then I hear one of my humans calling to me.

Step 1: Pretend you don't hear their first couple of calls. During this time it's actually important to move further away from them. (They really LOVE when I do this.)

Step 2: After one of their calls, stop in your tracks and look directly at them. This helps them know that you finally heard them. It gives them confidence.

Step 3: When they call your name again, start toward them. BUT, do not go in a straight line. We must teach humans that there is more than one way to go from point A to point K. Yes, a direct, non-stop straight line works. But zig-zagging to take in points B, C, D, E, F, G, H, I and J is soooooo much more fun! Plus this lets us investigate all sorts of interesting sights and smells. Oh, but you already knew that.

Simply be sure that this curvy route is gradually leading you to them. Humans eventually learn that straight lines are for losers. Most importantly, you are teaching them a skill that is important in their lives, too. There's more than one right way to do things! It's sort of like learning to color OUTside the lines!

Oh! One other thing... when you do get back to them, be sure to have on your happiest face. It's very difficult for humans to scold us when we are looking so happy AND when we are trying "so hard" to listen to them. Hee hee! I mean, woof!

18

RING MY BELL

We can learn some great training tips from each other. So, share brothers and sisters! One friend of a dog pal of mine even taught his humans to answer the doorbell to let him inside. Seriously.

My buddy, Baci, told me this story himself, so I know it's true.

The humans were at home one day when they heard the doorbell ring. They opened the front door, but no one was there. They went back to what they were doing. The doorbell rang again. Again, they went to the door, opened it, and looked around. Still, no one was there. Their dog was sitting there, but he didn't look alarmed in any way as if someone was hanging about playing tricks on the humans. Again, they closed the door. But this time, they stayed by the door to be ready to spring into action.

Sure enough, the doorbell rang. Without delay, they yanked the door open to see who it was.

They caught him red-pawwed. The dog stood on his back legs and rang the doorbell. They laughed and invited him back inside. From that day forward, this is how the dog let them know when he was ready to come inside.

So, try it on your humans. If you are too short to push the little button for the doorbell, try knocking on the door... or just bumping it firmly.

I've heard that they even sell bells to humans now to hang on doorknobs inside the house. This helps us train them to open doors for us whenever we need to pass through them. (Humans tend to forget to leave them open for us.)

My cat came up with his own techniques for getting back into the house. Typically he just presses his furry, fat face to the lowest window on a sliding glass door until a human sees him. But, if this isn't working, he climbs onto a chair on the porch which happens to be in front of a window. He starts out sitting on the chair staring at the human inside, which is The Ronald human, since the window is right beside his desk. If The Ronald human doesn't see him and get up to open the door for him, my cat literally knocks on the window. Jeeter will NOT be ignored.

The humans learn to let us in when we do these things. Otherwise... patience... persistency... just keep doing them until the human catches on to the training.

They do have a tendency to be busy stressing over work or some such thing. So, we are not only training them for a skill when we interrupt them, we are also improving their health. They need these breaks from stress regularly.

So, knock on the window or ring the doorbell or whatever works. They will learn. Most importantly, they learn that they should just pat us and stop fretting.

Frolicking with some friends, Ashley and Turner

19

PLAY TIME

Playing is one of the most important activities in life, but we should never play hard to get. That just builds up walls. The only time I believe that play is overrated is when it's at someone else's expense. (This is why humans get upset when we chew up one of their shoes.)

Actually, dogs have a keen sense of morality, so we are good at teaching humans to play fair in life. No cheating. No way. And we absolutely NEVER sit on people unless we like them.

I know that we can't always be playing. However, teach your humans that if you aren't actually playing, you can watch others play. Play actually brightens your day!

Thankfully, humans are fairly easy to train to play. The simplicity still manages to baffle them from time to time, however.

When you want them to play Fetch, pick up your ball or a stick, drop it at the human's feet, and look up longingly. Usually, on the very first try, they will pick it up and toss it away. Now it's super simple. Scamper over, pick it up again, and return the treasure to the humans. They'll toss it again.

This same approach works for Tug-of-War, too. Simply choose a favorite hunk of rope or stuffed animal and bring it to your human. Wag your tail gleefully as you crouch in front of them with a playful growl. If it fails to get them to play, try this next tip.

Look up to be sure you have their attention. Then shake the stuffed animal in your mouth with ferocious ferocity. Offer the toy to the humans once again, but don't completely let it go, of course. When they try to take it, pull it back a bit. The game is on!

Chase Me Chase Me is another easy game for humans to learn. They can play this both inside or outside. (Outside is way more fun because you can run in bigger, faster circles.)

Anyway, when your human approaches you, crouch the front half of your body very low, as if in a pounce position. Spread your front paws wide and be sure to wag your tail. When they get close to you, zoom right or left and run in a circle around them, encouraging them to follow. Now and then change directions to keep them interested.

It's also fun to sometimes let them get very close before zipping away again. This game ends when you are ready for a hug and some laughter. Simply let them catch you. Wheee!

Our humans get great benefit from playing with us, because we are also teaching them the value of taking pleasure in the simple things. Life is better when it is less complicated.

If you have a kitty in your house, then you know that they play a little differently than we do. Jeeter has tried to teach me his favorite games, and I return the favor and teach him some of mine. I admit, there tends to be some confusion. It's actually easier to train our humans, because cats are very stubborn.

I offer one precaution on teaching your humans to play these and any games. Humans have a weird need to fake us out sometimes. Just when you think they're perfectly trained to play, they blank out.

For example, a good buddy of mine, Baci (pronounced sort of like BAW-chee), is a fun, furry Golden Doodle. He loves to romp and play as much as any dog I know, and he's got his humans trained beautifully.

The Ronald photobombs Baci, Bandit and friend Peg

All the same, one afternoon, "it" happened. His Papa human came home from work. Baci immediately selected a favorite toy and scampered over to play. He did absolutely everything right, I tell you. His ears were perked up. He was grinning like crazy. He wagged his tail just as fast as he could.

And then his Papa human said those fateful words. You know… the ones we hate to hear. "It's time for a bath."

WHAT!?!?!

You must be kidding, Pop! Nope. Poor Baci. His jaw just dropped, along with his smile, his toy, his ears, and his tail. Talk about Heartbreak Hill.

Well, it worked out okay. His Papa human laughed and immediately saw the dread and disappointment on Baci's face. Okay. Okay. He had to have the bath and get fluffy and all that. But his Papa human knew that he'd blindsided poor Baci. He also knew that Baci needed some serious play time, so he got that, too.

Yeah, yeah, yeah. In addition to their trained skills, sometimes we must tolerate the weird whims of humans. We don't get it. But they think it's a bad thing to smell like a dog, so we have to take baths. Weird, I know.

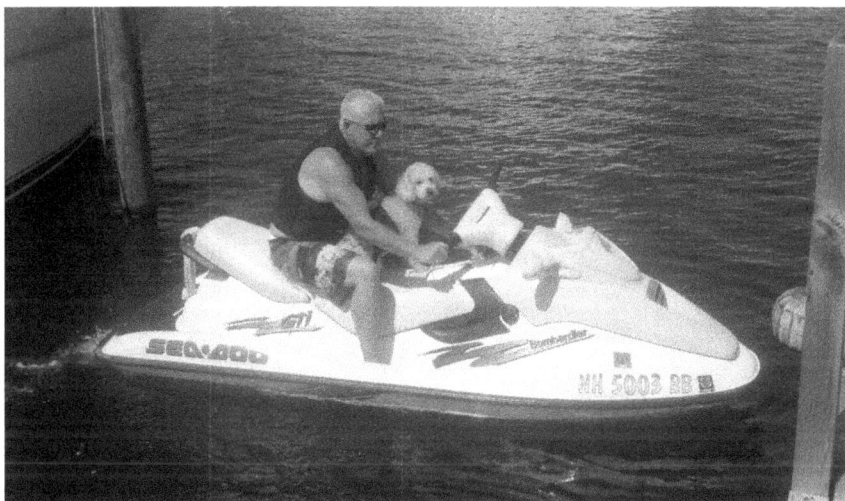

Baci, ready to jet-ski with his Pop, Al, a.k.a.Fred
(See, humans have confusion with their own names, too!)

20

TRAVELING FREEDOM'S ROADWAYS AND AIRWAYS

Hello! We are dogs! We love to travel. Anywhere. Anytime. When the pace picks up around my house, I know the humans are about to go someplace. Sometimes I get worried that they are not going to take me with them. Well, if there's a suitcase out, I get right on top so they know that I will fit, too. I guard it. I nap on top if necessary.

No, they've never put me in the suitcase, but I wouldn't mind... as long as I get to go wherever they're going. Heck, I've even trained my kitty to guard the suitcase any time I might have to leave my post to go get a cookie or something, and he doesn't even travel or like going for rides.

Usually, of course, there is no suitcase. I don't care if it's just going to be a five-minute trip. I dutifully hop into my travel bag without even being asked. Then, when they go looking for me, I've surprised them. I'm all ready to go. I mean it's my car seat, so I know it's going with them. I may as well already be in it. They can't forget me! Not that they ever would. I am unforgettable, after all... as we all are!

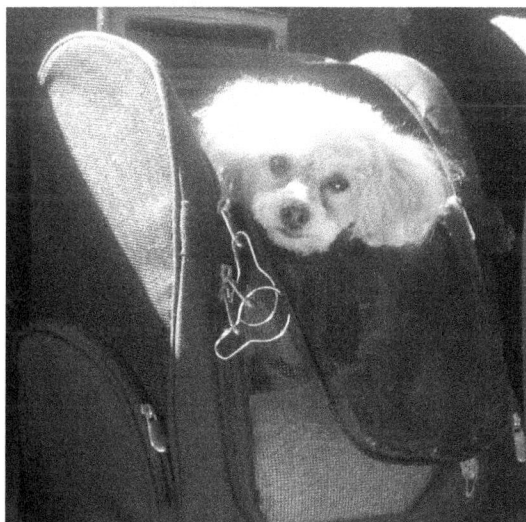

Some humans are just getting into the "appreciate Nature" thinking. We, on the other hand, have always loved the view. There is nothing like a little wind in the face to feel ourselves living!

Sometimes humans quip that we look silly poking our faces out the windows of cars as we zoom along. Hello again! We don't care if we look silly. In fact, silly is awesome! They really should try it more often.

I find that cats don't like it when they get caught looking silly or undignified. And, oh my! My cat lays around in some pretty funny positions.

What?!?

We canines truly don't care. Life is fun. What's dignified got to do with it? Our humans would be much happier if they stopped caring so much about what everyone else thought about how they appear.

Okay, humans do tend to go overboard and test our patience with all sorts of silly costumes and sweaters and booties and such. I've been dressed up as everything from a pirate to a mountain goat.

In reality, whether we look awesome or silly is of little consequence. We are getting attention. THAT, my dear, is the best.

I must mention a tiny little dog I met during this crazy, huge event at New Hampshire's Lake Winnipesaukee. They call it Laconia Bike Week, and there are hundreds of thousands of motorcycles everywhere. It's loud, but fun... with lots of dogs.

I met one big, tough dude, all dressed in his black leather and studs, along with his dog. Woah! His dog was even smaller than I am!

This guy wore a leather pouch on his hip, and his dog rode inside it, even on the motorcycle. He dressed his pup in his own leather helmet and doggles! So cool! Doggles kept his vision clear while they zoomed along. He wore them every day!

I wear a harness, rather than just a collar, every day. I always have. It carries my bling, er, uh, I mean, my ID tags. So, Baby, don't mess with it. Whether your bling is on a harness or a collar, I'm sure you know what I mean.

It makes me crazy when my humans say things like, "It's time for a bath," because I know they'll be removing my harness and the attached bling. I can't have my stuff back until I'm dry and fluffy again. Not good.

Well, at least I know I've got them trained to give it back... unlike when I'm trying to travel through an airport. This tends to be very hairy.

I understand that we need airport security measures, but must they always make me remove my harness? Not only must it be removed, but they then take my harness and put it on a conveyer belt that vanishes into a giant, long black box.
Oh, no!

Thank goodness it has always come out the other side. My Cathy human waits with me. TSA agents seem to struggle with my harness and how they can best get it back on me.

Here we go... an on-the-spot training opportunity. Okay, team. This one's simple. Just hold my harness with my leash ring on top and my bling tags dangling in front of me. I'll do the rest.

Hoppin' into my harness

Yup! They're amazed that I'll just poke my head through the collar portion and stand perfectly still while any human re-hooks the fastening clip. I then show them how I immediately hop into my travel bag, sit up handsomely, and grin at them. They smile back at me and laugh. "That was easy," they say.

Be prepared to have to train airport personnel every single time you travel, however. Somehow, my tips haven't made it into their training manuals. So, on every trip, I demonstrate yet again how easily we canines hop back into our gear and our travel bags.

These new humans always smile and marvel at how well behaved I am.

Well, yes! I <u>like</u> to travel with my humans. If I wasn't well-behaved, they might leave me at home. That just wouldn't fly well with me!

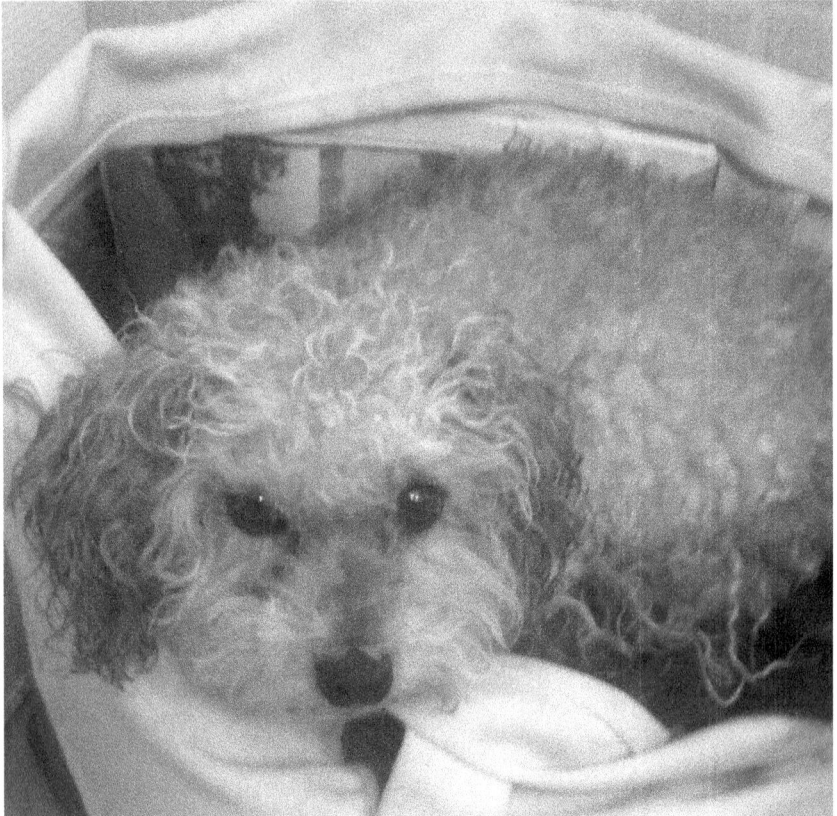

So, hang in there. There are LOTS of airports and thousands more airport personnel. Our training efforts never end.

On the aircraft itself, I always show the attendants how sweet I am. I sit quietly in my bag under the seat in front of my human. It should be noted, however, that this is a courtesy on my part. My ticket prices have been going up, up, up… sometimes even higher than my human's tickets! One of these days, I'm going to get the seat for myself, and my human can sit under the seat in front of me. Yeah!

I just hope they have pillows. I really like to nestle into lots of pillows.

21

NEVER, NEVER, NEVER GIVE UP

I believe the famous human, Winston Churchill said something like that, although he used the expression to "never give in." I learned that I actually train my human more readily when I let him or her believe that I am giving in. This is clearly seen in playing tug-of-war, for example. Now and then, it's important to let the toy go, so your human thinks they "won." This encourages them to play more frequently.

That's different than never giving up. Never giving up has more to do with the way we think. Humans need to see our persistency and consistency to help them learn it, too.

When we sit patiently and stare at the door behind which we know our food is hiding, we are teaching our human what we want.

A cat doing the same thing, on the other hand, is actually trying to send a message or command to the human via mental telepathy. They have the right "cattitude," but they forget that humans are slow. We must start more simply.

Perspective is another big lesson that requires constant reinforcement. Humans have a tendency to get caught up in their own viewpoint, as if they are the only ones with correct thinking. They even spend silly energy ridiculing others who think differently. If you need an example, just look at the circus surrounding the Presidential political process in the United States. Why don't these humans ever seem to learn that putting someone else down is a low attempt at making themselves appear better? Ah, well. We will keep loving them and trying to help them become better people.

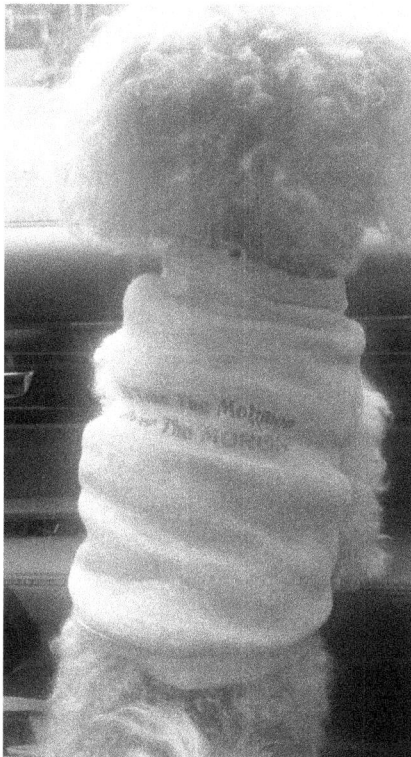

To teach them perspective, I share a lesson I've heard in a story a few times. (Go with me on this one; don't let the facts get in the way of a good story.) It's about that famously fabled King Arthur and his Knights of the Round Table.

In the center of the famed table stood an extremely large globe, representing the entire world as it was known at the time. The king asked each of his trusted, loyal knights to observe and explain what the world contained.

One pronounced that it was mostly water. Another quipped, "That's malarkey. I can clearly see huge land masses with mountains." "No," countered a third knight." "There is mostly desert."

From the far side of the table came the comment, "You are both silly. There is half water and half land." Another said, "There is mostly water but a bunch of islands." One protested, "There is a lot of land, but only a little water in the form of some lakes."

Then King Arthur asked all of his wise knights to stand up and move around the table and see the globe from other sides. He heard lots of "ooohs" and "ahhhs" and "ah-hahs" as each started to see what the others had been seeing.

This is exactly what happens when our humans take the time to see things from someone else's perspective or point of view. They end up expanding their own horizons, which is always a good thing.

*Perspective: I am less than half the size of my kitty,
unless I'm closer to the camera!*

When humans don't see things clearly or from the perspective we might wish they did, we must be extra patient. Help them see another view.

Sometimes you can do this by moving to a different area of the room. Choose to stretch out or curl up in a place that is out of the ordinary for you. When the human goes looking for you, they are surprised to not find you in one of your typically favorite spots.

They don't even realize you helped them expand their thinking, as they expanded their search. Enlarging our perspective expands our thinking. It's enlightening and refreshing.

I actually learned that little trick from my cat. Jeeter never quite understands why I enjoy sitting in my favorite places. Now and then he just can't stand it, so he tries them out. Well, he is more than twice my size, so he doesn't exactly fit very well in many of my spots. He sure looks funny though when he tries to squish his big, muscular body into the confines of one of my little daybeds. It does make the humans laugh out loud, which is always good.

Do these dog beds make me look fat?

I remember one particularly funny time when my human knew we were all in the bedroom, but she couldn't find the cat anywhere. She'd looked in the closet, under the bed, and on and behind all the furniture. It was as if Jeeter had vanished.

She called him. She noisily filled his food dish with crunchies... which normally brings him running. Still nothing. Finally, she happened to glance at my hard-sided travel crate, which I still like to lay inside from time to time while at home. There he was all comfortably scrunched inside, just watching her search for him. Of course, he didn't let on that he was watching and deliberately letting her search. This was all too entertaining.

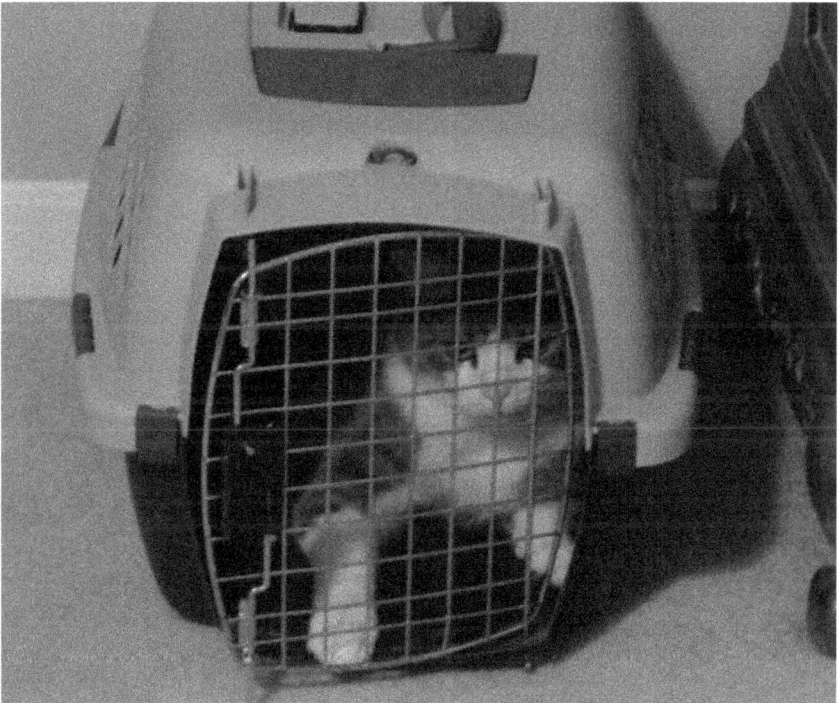

Jeeter has observed me with great curiosity while I'm in my crate. He never "gets" the big attraction, and he certainly had never before tested it out for himself. He had always looked at me through the door and said silly things like, "Don't worry little buddy. I'll spring you when the warden isn't looking."

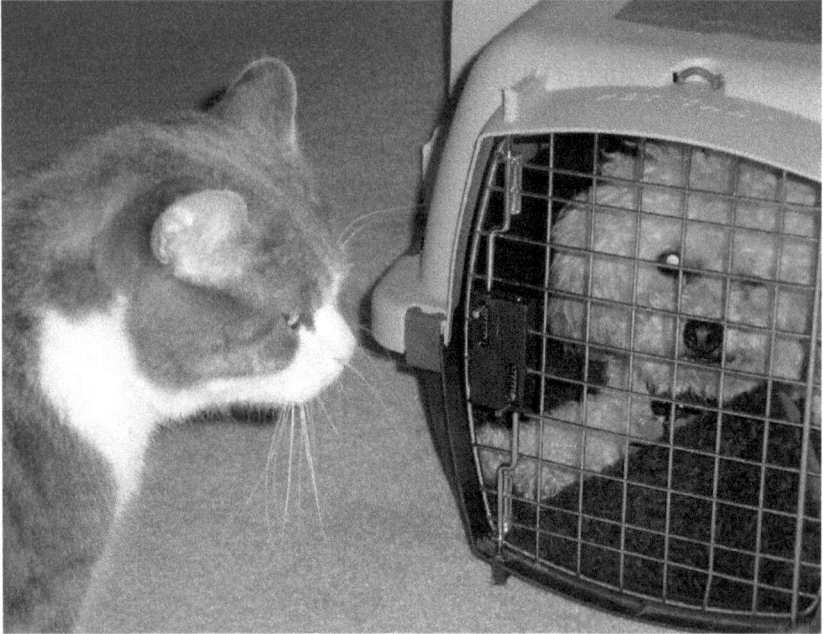

Well, he finally got his day and tested out my crate. Everyone shared a big laugh when my Cathy human's persistence finally paid off, and she found the kitty... inside my crate.

See, never, never, never give up.

22

RELAX ALREADY

Relaxation is a peculiar concept to many humans. Sometimes they really get it; other times, getting them to relax is a tough challenge. It's no challenge for me. Did I mention that I am a Pillow Puppy? That means, I don't care how soft a bed is, I prefer to be atop at least one pillow. My humans then developed yet another name for me. Princess and the Pea... I guess it's based on some fairytale. I don't care. Pillows rule!

Keeping us around improves their stress levels simply by our presence. It's true. Humans have even done studies that prove having a pet lowers blood pressure, reduces anxiety, and eases stress.

Some folks used to blame us for allergies and asthma, but now scientists have proven that families with pets actually have less risk of those ailments. This is important info for your human in these days of increasingly bad air quality. There are so many pollutants out there. Our existence in their homes helps keep them healthier. For those that don't believe, they can always get dogs that are hypo-allergenic, like I am. They've found that breeding dogs with poodles helps with this, as poodle hair must be clipped. We don't shed.

Oh, and dogs are awesome for therapy for all sorts of things… from early detection of seizures, low blood sugar and diabetic shock to cancers and anxiety. We are also extremely therapeutic for senior citizens. We provide friendship and companionship and a very important sense of purpose as they care for us. We truly do deliver health and happiness.

And did I mention we are also great chick magnets? Forget online dating sites... walk the dog!

Walking with Caroline, one of my "chicks"

Okay, okay… I digress. It's all about helping our humans to relax. I regularly try to demonstrate how sweet it is to stretch out and relax. On your back. On your belly. It doesn't matter. Just show them as often as possible. (In between play times and feeding times, of course.)

When they resist, you can go beyond demonstration and actually lay down on their feet. This always gets their attention. Teaching your humans to relax properly is vital to their healthy, long lives. Seriously. Take my Poppy human, for example. The Ronald started having lower back pains… it hurt for him to sit or stand up.

He borrowed a back stretching device from one of his human friends. This was to help him relax his spine, I think.

We were at the lake, and my Cathy human placed a towel out on the cool grass so he could lie down on it. No problem. Right? Wrong. My buddy Baci had to stretch out beside my human to show him that it was AOK to relax on the ground.

The Ronald getting help from Bacherooo!

Just because <u>we</u> know these things as bottom-line basics, never presume your humans know the same things. Sometimes they require a simple demonstration.

Another technique that really seems to work well is to literally lie down on top of your human. I don't care how large you are on the outside; inside there is a lapdog. If you don't dare do that, stretch out so that your body is pressed against their body just as snugly as possible. If they try to stir, put one paw out on them to block their exit.

Another good tip is keeping your eyes half closed when you look up at them. If they think that we are half asleep, they are more hesitant to disturb us. Or get them to sit in a sun spot. Mmmmmm... That nice warm sunshine will help them nap every time. Hee hee!

23

LOVE UNCONDITIONALLY

Loving unconditionally comes naturally to canines. We know and practice some love basics... We forgive and forget. We never hold grudges. We share love freely. We express love daily. We are always empathetic. We tune into feelings, not words. We deliver loyalty, unabashed.

These are natural skills for us, but we must always endeavor to share our example with humans. Remember, they usually mean well, but they tend to be slow learners. If they only understood the value of unconditional love to their health! Such positive energy increases quality and length of life, plus reduces stress. Now <u>that</u> is something always at the top of a human's "to do" list.

Even folks who might think they don't care much for dogs will love us, if we give them a chance to learn there's no greater love than puppy love! Okay, maybe I'm biased, but getting them to love a puppy is a wonderful place to start.

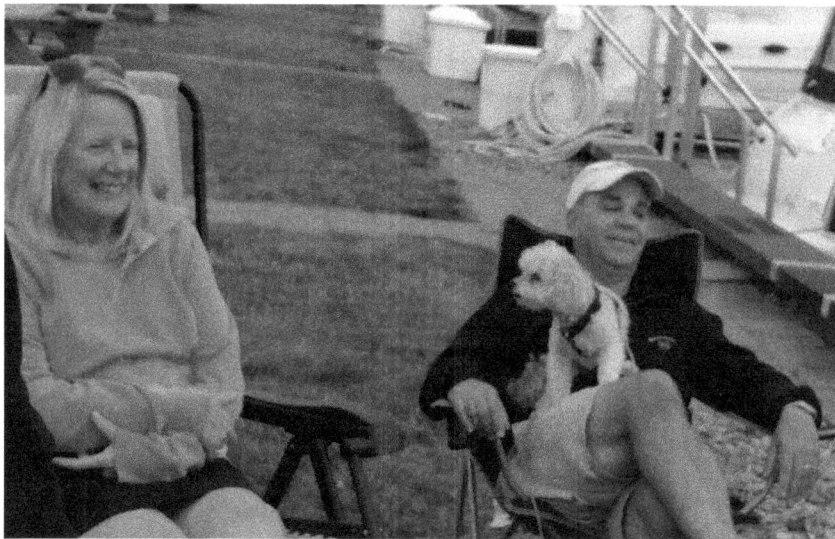

With my buddies Kathy and Bill Andrews

Often people who aren't always the easiest to love are the very ones who truly need love the most. As we know, and our humans can learn, love is a choice... a decision. It only starts out as a "feeling."

Feelings are fleeting. Humans get goofy sometimes and think feelings are supposed to stay forever. They typically have yet to learn that love (just as with most emotions) is a choice we make every single day. We always feel love because we make that decision. They can, too! Making this decision, this choice, every day will help them be more like us. And that IS a good thing. Like their favorite canine, humans can learn to let annoyances pass, to respect each other, to be kind, and to be faithful. Have confidence in your human. They can do it.

People deserve a second chance, which is one reason we never hold a grudge. If they catch on, they'll know that forgiveness is a gift they actually give to themselves. They sometimes think that forgiving someone is for that someone. They overlook how great it will feel inside themselves.

Help your human step out of their shell and stop living with a heavy heart. They get all caught up in life's little stresses and frustrations. Some humans even carry all this anger around in their hearts and then wonder why there's no room for love. As we pooches know, there's nothing gained by living with a clenched paw… even emotionally.

Keep forgiving until they learn to forgive themselves.

It helps to take even more time than usual to share your compassion with your humans. Cuddle and support them tirelessly, especially when they're down or in need. Let them know you understand.

When they see us living this way, expecting and demanding nothing in return, even the most stubborn humans start to catch on and live with more love in their hearts!

We also know how to cherish those we love. Unlike humans, dogs never take anyone for granted. That's why we always get so excited to see our humans.

Get real! When they leave, we don't know for sure that they will be back, even though they say they will. We can only hope that we'll see them again. That's why we never let them leave with anger or an argument hanging in the air. No way.

Even when they use angry words or express negative moods, we will not be brought down to their level. We have a higher responsibility... to help elevate them to the loving, wonderful, happy humans they are meant to be. We love our humans. We never forget that nothing is guaranteed to last even one more day.

Keep this in mind when you hear humans say weird things like, "You're acting like an animal." Or "You dog, you!" I mean, they say this as if it's a bad thing. Silly humans.

24

HAPPILY EVER AFTER

The growing older thing can be a drag. Except for the benefits. I mean, elders are given the softest pillows. (As I've mentioned, pillows are awesome!) Our elders get respect. Everyone seeks wisdom from our elders. And no matter how old we get, there's always someone older, to whom we should pay attention.

A great way of letting your humans know that we are listening and trying very hard to understand them is to tilt our heads. I wish that they would do this sometimes, so we'd know they are listening, too.

I've often heard my Ronald human say, "God gave us two ears and only one mouth, so we should listen twice as much as talk." Well, did you know that even in elder years, dogs can teach humans to be much better listeners? It's true. This is a very highly developed skill in dogs. We have some 206 facial expressions. 200 of them are with our ears. I'd like to see our humans match THAT!

Regardless of whether our humans are talkers or listeners, we believe in our humans no matter what. We are dogs.

We will stay with our humans in good times and bad, in sickness and health. We will lay by their side no matter what. If we can teach our humans to do the same for us, it is a miracle of love. In the end, stay with a loved one until it's totally over, no matter how difficult it is to watch them suffer.

If we are passing before them, pray that they have the strength to do the same. The endings always come too soon, but they become happy endings if we focus on the wonderful life and times we shared.

Also, humans sometimes say silly things, like "dogs don't think." Scheeeez! I believe that deep inside they know better. We not only think, we love, and we never forget.

If something wasn't pleasant, we forgive. Remember, never hold a grudge. But we often are very lucky and live lives that are filled with delightful memories. Let your humans know that you cherish those memories forever and ever. It's what we do. We always help our humans celebrate holidays. It's not that we know Valentine's Day from Thanksgiving, but we live every day knowing it's a special day. Now THAT is a wonderful skill to share with our humans.

Helping my original Mom celebrate

John Gehrisch, a very dear friend of my humans, has always loved dogs. My Newfoundland buddy, Miles, included a poem by John in the book he wrote, called "Dog Days in the Life of the Miles-Mannered Man." John loved having the tribute to his dog, also named "Bandit," published by Miles.

Years later, John lost Bogie, another very special dog pal. My Cathy human sent him a copy of Miles' book, which actually has a chapter with a very funny story about Bogie.

John planned to save reading the book for an upcoming road trip, but then he couldn't wait and started reading.

Later, he wrote to my Cathy human and said, "I have been so sad losing Bogie. I have felt he deserved to be immortalized somehow, but did not know how. You did it for me in a way I could never have matched or done better. From the bottom of my heart......**THANK YOU SO MUCH!!** This is something I will show many people proudly!"

John also shared how much the whole book made him laugh and cry, with so many happy memories that relate to all dogs. My Cathy human always seems to know just what to say. She wrote back to John, saying, "Tears for Bogie are splashes of happy memories... reflected in the longing in your heart. Never fear them."

Try to remember that whether our humans or our dog pals depart first, it's always sad. But no one can ever take away all the wonderful adventures and love we shared.

Helping Jeeter open a package

Once we are loved, we are truly Furrever Dogs. Be happy and hug your human today.

Bandit on board

EXTRA TREAT #1

FOOD & TREAT SAFETY

We're not talking about overspending here; this is about teaching your humans to save your life! Probably most of us have been guilty of eating the wrong things, but we also must teach our humans not to offer some items to their favorite furry beasts... EVEN WHEN WE BEG MOST ADORABLY. They think they are giving us a treat, but they are likely giving us a tummy ache, at the very least. So, go ahead and tear out these pages. This Extra Treat of vital information should be left somewhere where your humans will see it.

Damage caused by some items, such as onions, is cumulative. So, a little in last night's table scraps might not be such a big deal, right? Wrong. Because there may be a little more evilness than they realized... in the form of onion powder, or raw scraps while onions were being chopped, etc.

Keeping us safe and healthy is one of the most important ways that our humans show they love us! We show them love ALL the time.

I've seen many lists, but with lots of differences from list to list. I am one who'd rather be safe than sorry. So, here is an accumulated listing, gathered from my knowledge gained from my trusted veterinary staff at the Bedford Animal Hospital, and the following websites:
www.webMD.com
www.dogs.about.com
www.ASPCA.com
and the Pet Education site from www.DrsFosterSmith.com

There are many more sites, so I thought it might be helpful to compare lists. I learned a lot. For example, I've always had a great deal of confusion over which herbs, spices, and flavorings would be most important to avoid as pets. I had heard that cinnamon was bad, but it turns out that in small amounts it is just fine, along with other more traditional things like sage and mint. Nutmeg, on the other hand, is considered very bad... in any amount. That makes it extra important not to give us a human-type cookie or other sweet that could very well contain some ill-advised flavoring.

Most of us know that table scraps are a BIG no-no though we want them in a BIG yes-yes way. Our humans are trying to do their best, and they do not realize that they are NOT doing us a favor, nor are they "spoiling" us with such things as the extra fat they cut off the meat they just ate or a bite of buttery biscuit that they passed coyly under the table to our gleefully awaiting mouths. Healthy pets need healthy diets. Unhealthy is the only way to describe diets with too much fat, or sugar, or salt... for humans or us critters.

One bite may be no big deal to a human, but to a dog, especially a small dog, or a cat, that one bite is the size of a meal. It probably should be called "supersized."

WebMD reported 100,000 cases of pet poisoning in the United States of America just last year. The ASPCA details a full 25% of emergency calls they received last year alone were because a pet had just gobbled up some human medication, frequently ibuprofen and acetaminophen. No matter what the medicine may be... human or pet... our humans need to keep them safely out of our reach.

Some items we critters may consume will cause varying symptoms and degrees of risk. These depend a lot on the quantity consumed, our individual size, and our personal constitution and sensitivity. Regardless, no one who loves their animals wants us to suffer indigestion, breathing difficulties, diarrhea, weakness, or vomiting, never mind kidney or liver damage, coma, or death.

So, let's look at a basic list to share with your humans. This certainly does not contain every single item, but it does give you a strong starting point.

Human and Pet Medications
- Ibuprofen
- Acetaminophen
- Anti-depressants
- Prescriptions of any sort
- Pet Medicines for Flea & Tick (Many of these are for external use only and are poisonous if ingested!)

Chemical Poisons
- **Rat or Mouse poison** — We don't have to eat the poison itself; we simply have to take a bite of the mouse that did!
- **Heavy metals** – This includes such things as lead paint, linoleum (as in tiles), batteries, and zinc (in pennies).
- **Household cleaners** – Alert your humans to clean up any spilled bleach or ammonia right away. Also they need to keep such items as drain or pine cleaners, laundry detergent, and glue far away from us and any places we might step on them with our feet.
- **Personal Care items** – Some humans think it looks cute, but they should never let us pets get into nail polish or polish remover.
- **Garage or other stored items** — All lawn & garden fertilizers, turpentine paint thinner, putty, and pool

chemicals need to be far out of reach. They should also be sure motor oil, antifreeze, battery acid, and kerosene are stored safely. If humans read labels on insecticides they'll be certain they are specifically safe for pets. Remember, we wash our feet with our tongues and will consume all the chemicals we walked on during each outing. Yuk!

Plants

I'd heard about this decades ago with regard to cats and some dangerous house plants such as Philodendron, but the list of items that are bad is quite lengthy and includes some common varieties:

- Aloe
- Amaryllis
- Apple seeds, stems & leaves
- Azaleas
- Chrysanthemum
- Daffodils
- Daisies
- English Ivy
- Fox Glove
- Hosta
- Hyacinth
- Iris
- Lily of the Valley
- Marijuana / Hashish
- Mistletoe
- Oleander
- Philodendron
- Pothos
- Rhododendrons
- Tobacco
- Tulips

Human Foods

- **Alcohol** — No, it's not funny to get us drunk. Our systems are much smaller than theirs and react very badly to alcohol poisoning.
- **Caffeine** – Keep critters away from coffee, cocoa, tea, soft drinks, and caffeine pills.
- **Chocolate** – The darker the chocolate, the more deadly to us, their beloved pets.
- **Grapes & raisins** – cause kidney failure
- **Fruit pits** – such as cherry, peach, plum, and apple seeds
- **Citrus peels or seeds** – cause irritation and damage the central nervous system
- **Garlic** – including garlic powder
- **Mushrooms** – some varieties, including those common in backyards
- **Onion** – including onion powder
- **Tomatoes** – especially for cats
- **Yeast dough** – causes wretched stomach pain
- **Nuts** – cause vomiting, diarrhea, pancreatitis
- **Avocado** – causes cardiovascular damage

Difficult to digest (causing vomiting, diarrhea, and other digestive upsets), though not poisonous:
- Bones
- Corn cobs
- Dairy products
- Fats (even fat trimmings from meat, cooked or raw)
- Coconut water (too high in potassium)
- Large amounts of fish (small amounts only for dogs)
- Hops – as in beer
- Raw eggs
- Salt
- Sugars and sugary foods

There are several emergency numbers you may want to keep handy as help is available 24/7:

(These numbers/rates are effective as of 2016.)
ASPCA.org Poison Control Center   888-426-4435 ($65)
Pet Poison Helpline.com   855-764-7661 ($49)
National Animal Poison Control   800-548-2423 ($30)
Animal Poison Helpline.com   800-213-6680 ($39)
Kansas State University Veterinary Teaching Hospital
                                      1-785-532-5679 (FREE)

While most of these lines charge fees, in an emergency, these may seem like a pretty small price to pay to keep from poisoning us. Humans should also find out where the 24-hour veterinary service providers are in their local area. Get your humans to keep those numbers on the same list.

EXTRA TREAT #2

MORE SECRETS TO HAPPINESS

I took great pleasure sneaking in a few genuine Secrets to Happiness throughout the chapters. We canines have been pawsitively sure of these for generations. So, we hope you enjoyed our touching on some of these gems… from living by kindness and sharing enthusiastically to playing more, loving unconditionally, and never giving up. Now here are a few more to ponder. Again, though we dogs already love living by these secrets, share them with your humans for an even happier and more fulfilled life.

Happiness comes from the inside, not from something nice someone else does for us. Why be miserable when you can choose to be happy?

It's okay to be bad at something. Like, I am bad at climbing trees. Okay, I can accept that. There is no shame in not knowing or not having all the answers. We do not have to be perfect; just being perfectly real is best.

Money does not buy happiness. Sure, we might get better toys and treats, but humans should learn from dogs and be happy with hugs. Stuff brings pleasure. Love brings happiness.

Don't be a jerk. No one will ever see a dog exhibit a snarky attitude or exhibit road rage. We never curse out anyone or even have the urge to flip them the middle paw.

Humans should follow their guts, just as dogs follow their noses, especially when it leads them in a zig-zag pattern.

Live in the now. Be grateful for each moment. Recognize that most frustrations and anxieties come from pondering the past or living in the uncertainty of the future. Worry is worthless.

Accept yourself. Never be ashamed of being "you!"

Run away from toxic people. Relationships matter. If someone is hell-bent on being hateful or hurtful, run away and don't look back. (It matters not how long you've known them or how good they claim they have been to you.)

Be the best friend you wish to have. That's why dogs have so many friends. Dogs never isolate themselves from others nor compromise their integrity.

Live out loud! Whether something is great or needs improvement, don't be afraid to speak out.

Spend some time alone with yourself every day, even if it's just a few minutes basking in a favorite sun spot.

Humans often talk to dogs; humans should listen, too.

When a dog has passed from your life, relish the happiness and glee he dedicated his life to bringing to you.

EXTRA TREAT #3

GREAT RESOURCES

While we pups are never sure when websites change or just how accurate or up-to-date information there is, we're listing a wide variety of sources here for your enjoyment. For simplicity, we have left off the www and https prefixes. For example: HumaneSociety.org

TRAINING
Cesar Milan – Dog Whisperer   cesarsway.com
The Association of Professional Dog Trainers apdt.com
DogsBestFriendTraining.com
NaturalDogTraining.com

BREEDS
Petfinder.com
AKC.org/dog-breeds
Dogtime.com
Breeders.net
DogBreedInfo.com
AnimalPlanet.com/breed-selector
PuppyFind.com
Purina.com/dogs/dog-breeds
DogBreedsList.info

HEALTH & SAFETY
Pets.WebMD.com/dogs
PetMD.com
DogHealth.com
DogKinetics.com
WebVet.com
Vet.Cornell.edu

ADOPTION
ASPCA.org
AllPaws.com
AnimalWelfareSociety.org
AdoptAPet.com
The ShelterPetProject.org
Petfinder.com
RescueMe.org

TRAVEL
PetMovers.com
WeMovePets.com
DogTravelCompany.net
PetTravelCenter.com
PetsWelcome.om
PetTravel.com
TripsWithPets.com
DogFriendly.com
TakeYourPet.com
BringFido.com
GoPetFriendly.com
PetFriendlyTravel.com
TravelDogsAustralia.com
OfficialPetHotels.com
DogTime.com
AAA.com/Petbook

MISC – Food, behavior, nutrition, and more
Whole-Dog-Journal.com
Dogster.com
DogTime.com
PetDiets.com
DoggieBuddy.com
PetUniversity.com
Pets.WebMD.com/dogs

CAREERS FOR DOG LOVERS

Living with us is simply not enough for some dog fans. Here are just a few of the dog-related careers to help them consider. Go ahead. Inspire your human's future thinking.

American Kennel Club Staff
Animal Control Officer / Humane Officer
Animal Hospital Attendant
Animal Hospital Groundskeeper
Animal Hospital Bookkeeper
Animal Hospital Receptionist
Animal Rights Lawyer
Animal Shelter Staff

Boarding Kennel Attendant

Dog Behaviorist
Dog Breeder
Dog Chef
Doggie Daycare Worker
Dog Groomer
Dog ID & Rescue
Dog Illustrator
Dog Massage Therapist
Dog Park Worker
Dog Photographer
Dog Product Inventor
Dog Product Manufacturer
Dog Product Retailer
Dog Psychologist
Dog Show Handler
Dog Show Judge

Dog Therapist
Dog Trainer
Dog Transportation Specialist
Dog Walker
Dog Writer

Nature Reporter

Pet Adoption Counselor
Pet Communicator
Pet Sitter
Pet Supply Worker
Police / Military K-9 Units
Pooper Scooper
Professional Field Trialers
Public Service Worker Dog Handler

Service Dog Trainer

Therapy Dog Handler

Vet Assistant
Veterinarian
Veterinary Science & Research
Vet Tech
Volunteer

...And some related websites to get you started:
NationalDogGroomers.com
AnimalBehavior.org   Animal Behavior Society
PetSitters.org   National Association of Pet Sitters
Abka.com   American Boarding Kennels Association
NACANET.org   National Animal Control Association
ASPCA.com   American Society for the Prevention of Cruelty
to Animals
PPA.com   Professional Photographers of America

GAG.org   The Graphic Artist Guild
DogWalker.com
APAWS.org   Association of Professional Animal Waste
Specialists
IAAMB.org   International Association of Animal Massage &
Bodywork

ACKNOWLEDGEMENTS

One final word... I could not have published this book without the help of some very important humans. First, my Cathy human who keyed all my lessons and lingo into the computer for me. A special thank you to those of you who shared special stories, training tips, and photographs for me to use, too, including Patte Powers, Al and Peg Marracco, Bob and Glenna Burnham, Keira Martin, June Gulumian, my Bedford Animal Hospital docs, techs and groomer, my fans at St. Mark Village, and all my other human friends who love dogs! Here's woofin' at you!

Are you ready for some football?

Remember to check out my Cathy human's website, www.GoodLiving123.com where she lists all her books and audiobooks, plus dishes up more great info, stories, and free articles... all to help make good living as easy as 1 – 2 – 3.

MORE PHOTOS FOR MY FANS

With my original Mom!

Oh, yeah… Jeeter's got Dad's remote control… again!

Jeeter helping make a Minnie Mouse costume

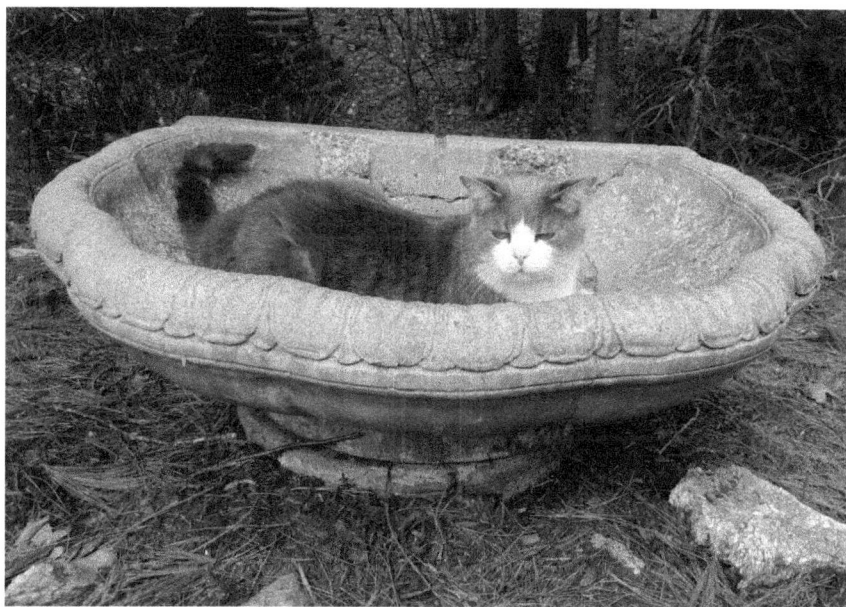

Jeeter doesn't "get" why the birds won't come to him

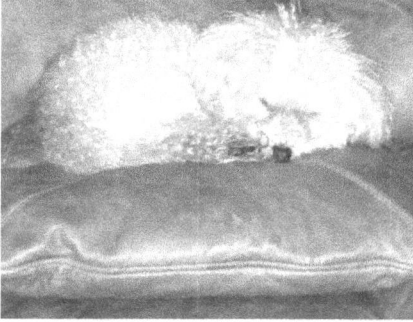

Perhaps I mentioned that I am a Pillow Puppy!

www.ingramcontent.com/pod-product-compliance
Lightning Source LLC
Chambersburg PA
CBHW072021040426
42447CB00009B/1680